Heidegger Explained

IDEAS EXPLAINED™

Hans-Georg Moeller, *Daoism Explained*

Joan Weiner, *Frege Explained*

Hans-Georg Moeller, *Luhmann Explained*

Graham Harman, *Heidegger Explained*

IN PREPARATION

David Detmer, *Sartre Explained*

Rondo Keele, *Ockham Explained*

Paul Voice, *Rawls Explained*

David Detmer, *Phenomenology Explained*

David Ramsay Steele, *Atheism Explained*

Rohit Dalvi, *Deleuze and Guattari Explained*

MARTIN HEIDEGGER

Heidegger Explained

From Phenomenon to Thing

GRAHAM HARMAN

OPEN COURT
Chicago and La Salle, Illinois

Volume 4 in the Ideas Explained™ Series

This book has been reproduced in a print-on-demand format from the 2007 Open Court printing.

To order books from Open Court, call toll-free 1-800-815-2280, or visit www.opencourtbooks.com.

Open Court Publishing Company is a division of Carus Publishing Company.

Printed and bound in the United States of America.

Library of Congress Cataloging-in-Publication Data

Harman, Graham, 1968-
    Heidegger explained : from phenomenon to thing / Graham Harman.
        p. cm. — (Ideas explained ; v. 4)
    Summary: "Presents a summary of the philosophy of Martin Heidegger (1889-1976), and gives an account of Heidegger's life and career" — Provided by publisher.
    Includes bibliographical references and index.
    ISBN-13: 978-0-8126-9617-2 (trade paper : alk. paper)
    ISBN-10: 0-8126-9617-4 (trade paper : alk. paper)
    1. Heidegger, Martin, 1889-1976.   I. Title.
`B3279.H49H274 2007
193—dc22
                                                        2007005899

Contents

Preface   ix

Introduction   1

1. BIOGRAPHY   5

Early Life   5
Rising Star   7
The Hitler Era   10
Life after WWII   11
Appearance and Character   13

2. A RADICAL PHENOMENOLOGIST   15

Husserl's Phenomenology   16
1919: Heidegger's Breakthrough   20
1920–21: Facticity and Time   24
1921–22: The Triple Structure of Life   28
1923: Being in the Public World   32

3. MARBURG   37

1925: The Dragon Emerges   38
1927: Temporality and Being   44
1928: Human Transcendence   50

4. *BEING AND TIME*   55

The Question of Being   57
Tools and Broken Tools   60
Fallenness and Care   66
Death, Conscience, and Resoluteness   71
Dasein's Temporality   73

5. FREIBURG BEFORE THE RECTORATE 79
   1929: Nothingness 80
   1929–30: On Boredom and Animals 84
   1930: Veiling and Unveiling 91

6. A NAZI PHILOSOPHER 95
   1933: The Rectoral Address 97
   1933–34: Actions as Rector 100

7. HERMIT IN THE REICH 105
   1935: Inner Truth and Greatness 106
   1935: Earth and World in the Artwork 109
   1936: The Echo of Hölderlin 112
   1936–38: The Other Beginning 117
   1940: The Metaphysics of Nietzsche 123

8. STRANGE MASTERPIECE IN BREMEN 127
   The Thing 129
   The Enframing 135
   The Danger 138
   The Turn 139

9. THE TASK OF THINKING 143
   1950: Language Speaks 143
   1951–52: We Are Still Not Thinking 146
   1955: Releasement 149
   1963–64: The End of Philosophy 151

10. HEIDEGGER'S LEGACY 157
    His Legacy Now 157
    Looking Ahead 160

Suggestions for Further Reading 165
Glossary 173
Appendix: Heidegger's Numerology 179
Index 185

Preface

This book explains the philosophy of Martin Heidegger in clear and simple terms, without footnotes or excessive use of technical language. The goal of this Open Court series is to present difficult philosophers in a way that any intelligent reader can understand. But even while aiming at clarity for a general audience, a book of this kind can do something more: by avoiding professional jargon and the usual family quarrels of scholars, it can bring Heidegger's philosophy back to life as a series of problems relevant to everyone. Since Heidegger is probably the most recent great philosopher in the Western tradition, to present his ideas to general readers means inviting them to witness the emerging drama of twenty-first century philosophy.

It is typical of great thinkers that they transcend their own backgrounds, political views, and historical eras, appealing even to those who do not share these factors. This is clearly true in Heidegger's case. Although he was a German steeped in local customs and folklore, his greatest influence has been abroad, in such places as the United States, Japan, the Arab world, and especially France. A committed Nazi who paid open tribute to Hitler, he still finds numerous admirers among communists and liberal democrats, and some of his greatest interpreters have been Jewish philosophers such as Hannah Arendt, Jacques Derrida, and Emmanuel Levinas. And although Heidegger's works can be viewed as arising from the general anxiety and antirationalist attitude in Germany following World War I, his ideas show no signs of losing their freshness even in the twenty-first century.

While Heidegger did not publish widely during his lifetime, he was a prolific writer, producing the equivalent of at least one book per semester throughout his academic career. The *Complete*

Edition of Heidegger's works, still being published by the firm Vittorio Klostermann in Frankfurt, is now projected to reach 102 volumes, and will probably go far beyond that number. Due to the vast number of Heidegger's works, I have sometimes had to make cruel decisions about what to exclude from the present book. As a general rule, I have left out most of Heidegger's detailed commentaries on past philosophers. There are two reasons for this. First, since the books in this series can assume no wide philosophical background among readers, it seemed unwise to devote many pages to explaining the philosophies of Plato, Leibniz, or Kant in a book on Heidegger that is short enough already. Second, I tend to agree with a small minority of commentators who find Heidegger somewhat overrated as a historian of philosophy. It is my view that Heidegger's readings of past philosophers are mostly of interest for what they tell us about Heidegger himself, and not for their historical value. I have made only two exceptions, since they are so central to Heidegger's career that it would be a distortion to omit them: namely, his readings from the 1930s of the poet Friedrich Hölderlin and the philosopher Friedrich Nietzsche.

If you are about to make your first encounter with Heidegger's philosophy, I envy you this moment, and would like this book to be a helpful guide that spares as many wrong turns as possible. For me, as for countless admirers of Heidegger's works, it is difficult to imagine how I would see the world today if he had never existed. The goal of this book is to lead readers toward a similar experience, perhaps summoning them to become active participants in the struggle to push Heidegger's insights even further. That story remains to be written. Perhaps one of the readers of this book will play a key role in writing it.

Introduction

The title of Heidegger's greatest book is *Being and Time*, and these three words explain the whole of his philosophy. It was his view that every great thinker has a single great thought. For Heidegger, that single thought can be expressed as follows: *being is not presence*. Being is not present, because *being is time*—and time is something never simply present, but constantly torn apart in an ambiguous threefold structure. The whole of Heidegger's career serves only to clarify the insight that being is not presence. The being of things such as candles and trees never lies fully present before us, and neither does being itself.

A thing is more than its appearance, more than its usefulness, and more than its physical body. To describe a candle or tree by referring to its outer appearance, or by concepts, is to reduce it to a caricature, since there is always something more to it than whatever we see or say. The true being of things is actually a kind of *absence*. A key term for Heidegger is "withdrawal": all things withdraw from human view into a shadowy background, even when we stare directly at them. Knowledge is less like seeing than like *interpretation*, since things can never be directly or completely present to us.

When Heidegger talks about time, he is not talking about something measured by a clock or calendar, but about a kind of temporality found even in a single instant. Consider Heidegger's famous example of a hammer, which we will examine in detail below. In one sense, a hammer remains invisible to us: we tend to use our tools without noticing them, and focus instead on the house or ship we are building. The hammer usually withdraws from view. But even when we notice it, such as when it breaks, the hammer will always be more than whatever we see or say about it.

1

This means that the being of the hammer is always absent; it labors silently in invisible depths, and is not "present-at-hand," to use Heidegger's term. But absence is only one side of the story. Hammers, candles, and trees cannot be only absent, because then we would never see anything or have any relations with anything at all. Yet quite obviously, the hammer is also present: I see its wooden handle and metallic head, feel its weight, and interpret it either as a tool for building, an item of hardware priced for sale, or a weapon for hand-to-hand combat. For a dog, a baby, an ant, or a parrot, most of the hammer's usual properties are not there at all, which shows that the presence of a thing is also determined by those who encounter it.

Putting these two sides of the story together, we find that the world is ambiguous, or two-faced. On the one hand, things hide from view and go about simply being whatever they are (which Heidegger calls "past"). On the other hand, things become present with certain characteristics through being *interpreted* as tools, weapons, or items of entertainment (which Heidegger calls "future"). Together, these two dimensions unite in a new kind of "present," since the world is dynamically torn between the being of things and the oversimplified surfaces through which they appear to us. The world is a constant passage back and forth, between shadow and light—and this endless passage is called time. With this simple idea, Heidegger inaugurates a revolution in human thought. He holds that the entire history of philosophy and science since ancient Greece has reduced objects to some form of presence, and has thereby missed the full richness of their reality. Modern technology, too, has stripped things of their mystery and reduced them to nothing but stockpiles of useful presence. Here we find one possible explanation for Heidegger's shocking support for the Nazi movement, which he claimed was the only force able to confront the dangerous technological worldview shared by American capitalism and Soviet communism.

But there is another central idea in Heidegger that most readers find convincing, though I myself find it mistaken. This is the notion that time belongs primarily to *human beings*, not to inanimate objects. The name for human existence in Heidegger's philosophy is Dasein (pronounced DAH-zeyn), a German word usually not translated into English. This term literally means "being-there," and is used in everyday German to refer to the existence of anything at all: whether humans, mushrooms, or chairs. But Heidegger restricts this term to human beings alone, since he believes that only humans truly exist in the world, fully open to it, whereas physical objects merely sit around in the world without having any access to it. He prefers the term Dasein because if we say "human being," we already have too many theories and prejudices in advance about what human being means: for example, we might already think of humans as rational animals, tool-making animals, highly advanced African apes, or mortal bodies inhabited by immortal souls. In order to exclude these prejudices from the discussion, Heidegger speaks of Dasein so that we focus only on those aspects of human being that can be displayed in a rigorous philosophical way. For Heidegger, only Dasein is temporal. Rocks and mountains can be viewed as merely present-at-hand physical objects, but in the case of human beings there is always a two-faced interplay of shadow and light, veiling and unveiling—the interplay known as time.

In this way, Heidegger follows the tradition of the great German thinker Immanuel Kant (1724–1804), still the dominant philosophical figure of our era. In 1781, the largely unknown Kant published his masterwork *Critique of Pure Reason*. According to this book, philosophy has no hope of discussing the way things are in themselves, since human beings only gain access to the world in a limited human way: for instance, we cannot know whether time and space exist independently of us, but can only say that they are conditions of possibility of all human experience. Humans will never know what lies outside the structure of human experience. After a brief delay, Kant's book struck Western philosophy like an earthquake, and the aftershocks continue more than two centuries later.

Heidegger remains loyal to this Kantian tradition in philosophy: he never tells us anything about the causal relationship between fire and cotton, but focuses on the *human* experience of temporality, on the veiling and unveiling of things encountered in the world by Dasein. The title *Being and Time* refers to the interplay between the veiled reality of things and their luminous but oversimplified appearance in what Heidegger calls the "clearing" of human existence, in reference to the occasional treeless spaces found along dark forest paths. This is Heidegger's entire philosophy in a nutshell; the rest is just commentary. The difficulty of his

writing style should not be allowed to conceal the unusual simplicity of his ideas.

Readers of this book may wish to have one of Heidegger's own
works on hand as well. My usual recommendation is *History of the
Concept of Time.* The name of this book is misleading, since the full
German title calls it the *preface* to a history of the concept of time,
and it never gives any history at all. It is actually an early version of
Being and Time, presented by Heidegger to his students at the
University of Marburg, and somewhat easier to understand than
his more famous book. *History of the Concept of Time* also gives us
Heidegger's clearest criticism of the philosophical school known as
phenomenology, founded by Edmund Husserl in 1900–1901.

The young Heidegger was widely regarded as Husserl's star
pupil, but eventually became the most radical critic and rebel
within his teacher's movement. For this reason, we will begin by
discussing phenomenology and Heidegger's own radicalized version of it. Phenomenology walls philosophy off from science by
asking us to forget every scientific theory about how the world
works, and to focus instead on a patient, detailed description of
how the world appears to us before we invent any theories. In our
everyday experience, we do not hear sound waves, but simply hear
a door slamming; the sound waves are just a scientific theory, no
matter how solid this theory may seem. Likewise, we do not actually see a can of sliced fruit, but only see one side of the can at a
time, while the existence of the rest of the can is merely assumed.
In other words, Husserl's phenomenology holds that things are
phenomena (appearances) for human consciousness. By contrast,
Heidegger claims that the being of things is not their presence at
all, since things are always partly withdrawn into shadow, and
exceed all visibility and all concepts we might have of them.

1

Biography

Early Life

Martin Heidegger was born on September 26, 1889, in Messkirch in southern Germany, a small town difficult to reach even today. The meaning of Messkirch in German is probably "Mass Church" (there is some dispute), and appropriately enough, the town is home to a magnificent Baroque church called St. Martin's. The philosopher's father was employed as sexton at the church, and the family lived in a small house that still faces it. Young Martin assisted in ringing the church bells, and was otherwise raised in an atmosphere of deep Catholic piety. In political terms, Messkirch was a stronghold of Catholic centrism, and during the 1920s would consistently register fewer votes for the Nazi Party than most other parts of Germany. For this reason, it would be mistaken to trace Heidegger's later Nazism to some sort of provincial small-town bigotry.

Martin's sister Marie was born in 1891 and died in 1956. For some reason she is often omitted entirely from biographies of the philosopher, though his letters show that they enjoyed warm interactions during his visits to Messkirch. Martin's brother Fritz was born in 1894 and died in 1980, and had an incalculable influence on Martin's life. Often portrayed as just a lovable country boy who kept his famous brother humble, Fritz Heidegger was in fact a remarkable figure. Removed from training for the priesthood due to a speech impediment, he eventually became a skilled local banker, a beloved orator of rare comic brilliance, and a prolific author of unpublished books of worldly wisdom. Fritz was entrusted with Martin

Heidegger's manuscripts during the most dangerous period of World War II, and worked selflessly to type them.

Given the limited finances of the Heidegger family, Martin needed the assistance of a Church scholarship to attend the Gymnasium (preparatory high school) in the nearby city of Konstanz. In 1906, he transferred to a Gymnasium in Freiburg near the Black Forest, his first contact with the city of his future glory. Another stroke of destiny occurred the following year, when Heidegger's early mentor Conrad Gröber, the future Archbishop of Freiburg, presented seventeen-year-old Martin with a book by the Austrian philosopher Franz Brentano, *On the Manifold Meaning of Being according to Aristotle*. This gift had a major impact on Heidegger's life. In the first place, it gradually led him toward Brentano's student Edmund Husserl, founder of the movement known as phenomenology, which Heidegger would later adopt and radicalize. But in a deeper sense, Brentano's book led the young student to wonder vaguely, "If being has several meanings, what is its most fundamental meaning?" The question of the meaning of being would eventually become Heidegger's trademark.

Two years later, in 1909, Heidegger entered the Jesuit novitiate in Tisis, Austria. A brilliant career as a Jesuit theologian seemed to lie in store. Yet within just a few weeks, he was discharged from training due to a heart condition (ironically, he would pursue an athletic lifestyle and live to the age of eighty-six). This incident began Heidegger's gradual alienation from the Catholic Church, culminating in a permanent break with the Church a decade later. With his brief Jesuit training ended, Heidegger turned toward his studies at the University of Freiburg, focusing on philosophy and theology. During these years, his continued interest in Brentano's philosophy led him to Husserl, whose masterwork *Logical Investigations* never seemed to be in demand at the university library, allowing Heidegger to borrow it repeatedly. To visualize the young Heidegger lost in the pages of Husserl's great book is to imagine one of the most dramatic scenes of twentieth-century philosophy. Heidegger is best understood as a heretical disciple of Husserl—a radical phenomenologist who overturned phenomenology and turned it into something entirely different.

Heidegger received his doctorate in 1913. The German academic system requires a further postdoctoral process known as *Habilitation* in order to become a university teacher. This includes another lengthy thesis beyond the Ph.D., which Heidegger completed in 1915 with an interesting work on the medieval philosopher Duns Scotus. In the meantime, World War I had broken out. Like the rest of his unlucky generation, Heidegger was called into service in this famously abysmal conflict. The continued questions surrounding his health excluded him from armed combat; he served instead in the postal censor's office, and at a meteorology station near Verdun.

In the immediate postwar years, the main elements of Heidegger's adult life began to take shape. In 1917 he married Elfride Petri, an economics student in Freiburg and the daughter of an enlightened Protestant military officer. The couple would have two sons: Jörg (in 1919) and Hermann (in 1920). At age fourteen, Hermann was told by his mother that his true biological father was not Martin Heidegger, but rather her childhood friend Dr. Friedel Caesar, a secret that Hermann loyally kept until it was made public in 2005. Due to Heidegger's increasing distance from Catholicism, the couple broke their promise to have the boys raised as Catholics. Meanwhile, in Heidegger's latest stroke of amazing philosophical luck, the newest professor of philosophy in Freiburg was none other than Edmund Husserl himself. Heidegger tried repeatedly to become a close associate of Husserl, but the older thinker viewed him at first as a "Catholic philosopher," and assumed that his strong religious commitments would prevent full openness to the radical questioning demanded by phenomenology.

In the winter semester of 1917-18, Husserl finally accepted Heidegger as his assistant. He grew deeply impressed by the talents of his apprentice, eventually coming to see him as an intellectual heir. As Husserl supposedly told Heidegger one day, "Phenomenology, that is you and me!" But the relationship gradually led to disillusionment. Heidegger's growing intellectual distance from Husserl beginning in the early 1920s was capped in the following decade by Heidegger's Nazi allegiances, while Husserl, Jewish by birth, was barred from university facilities.

Rising Star

Heidegger's own philosophical career began in 1919, with the so-called War Emergency Semester in Freiburg. In a lecture course now available in English as *Towards the Definition of Philosophy*, we find Heidegger's first original steps beyond Husserl's phenomenology. In 1920, he began an important friendship with the philosopher Karl Jaspers, bringing him the new experience of a friend roughly his own age and of somewhat comparable intellectual stature. This friendship too would sour during the Nazi period; Jaspers's wife was Jewish and faced genuine physical danger despite her husband's fame.

By the early 1920s, the youthful Heidegger was already a legendary teacher in Freiburg. But like his teacher Husserl, he had published far less than he had written, and this lack of publication had kept him stranded at the level of a mere instructor. Even so, his reputation for originality had reached the point that the Universities of Marburg and Göttingen both began to consider professorships for him. It was in the hilly central town of Marburg that the lightning struck. Heidegger accepted a professorship there in 1923, and would remain in Marburg for a brief but spectacular period until 1928, when he was called back to Freiburg as Husserl's successor. The half-decade in Marburg was no doubt the most important period of Heidegger's life, and one of the most illustrious chapters in the history of the city as well. It was during this time that Heidegger began to do philosophical work in his famous Black Forest hut in Todtnauberg. This was also the period of Heidegger's growing reputation among students as the "hidden king" of German philosophy, despite his continued lack of publications.

Semester by semester, Heidegger's Marburg lecture courses broke fresh ground and solidified his highly original vision of philosophy. There was an important friendship with the theologian Rudolf Bultmann, who would incorporate many of Heidegger's ideas into his own work. Still more importantly, there was his meeting with Hannah Arendt, later a brilliant political philosopher in her own right. In 1924, Arendt was still an eighteen-year-old Jewish student from East Prussia, a shy but forceful character who fascinated her fellow students no less than Heidegger, who was then a married professor of thirty-four. In February of 1924 they began a love affair. Although by no means the only affair of Heidegger's life, this one was so important to him that he once claimed Arendt was the inspiration for all his major works of the 1920s.

Foremost among these works was *Being and Time*, justly regarded as Heidegger's greatest achievement. Late in 1924, the conflicted Arendt left Marburg to study with Jaspers in Heidelberg. During the summer semester of 1925, despite the absence of his young muse, Heidegger gave the lecture course in Marburg now known in English as *History of the Concept of Time*— a lucid first draft of *Being and Time* prefaced by a brilliant survey of the achievements of Edmund Husserl, whom he both celebrates and surpasses. Heidegger was now on the doorstep of *Being and Time*, which like so many great works in the history of philosophy was published only due to external pressures. When the philosopher Nicolai Hartmann left Marburg for Cologne, his full professorship became vacant. The Marburg faculty favored Heidegger for the job, especially since Hartmann himself had spoken in glowing terms of an outstanding book in progress by Heidegger. The problem for the young philosopher, now as ever, was his lack of publications; his colleagues urged him to speed up the writing process.

In 1925, Heidegger was nominated by the Marburg faculty to fill the vacant full professorship. This suggestion was vetoed by the Ministry of Culture in Berlin, with a rejection letter stating that a chair as important as the one in Marburg should not go to someone with such a minimal publication record. In the summer of 1926, the Marburg faculty renewed its request, this time enclosing the galleys of Heidegger's new book. In one of the most embarrassing blunders in academic history, these pages were returned from Berlin marked "inadequate." Only in 1927, when Husserl's famous journal *Yearbook for Phenomenology and Phenomenological Research* included Heidegger's book in its pages, was Heidegger finally approved as Hartmann's successor.

He did not remain on the job for long. Already in 1928, Heidegger was summoned back to Freiburg as Husserl's successor, now a crowned king of philosophy rather than a hidden one. His return to Freiburg featured intriguing lecture courses such as the 1929–30 *Fundamental Concepts of Metaphysics* (on the unlikely twin themes of boredom and animals) and even more famous one-shot lectures such as *What Is Metaphysics?* (on the concept of nothingness). Many of the students who came to Freiburg to work with the aging Husserl were soon bewitched by Heidegger's magic instead. After the publication of *Being and*

Time, there were growing numbers of students from as far afield
as the United States and Japan. While the younger Heidegger had
already drawn such first-rate disciples as Arendt and Hans-Georg
Gadamer, his lectures of the late 1920s were attended by such
eventual key thinkers as Emmanuel Levinas of Lithuania and
Xavier Zubiri from the Basque region of Spain. In 1929, in Davos,
Switzerland, the newly famous Heidegger engaged in a debate on
the philosophy of Kant with Ernst Cassirer—an electrifying event
at the time, one that was attended or followed by virtually all
important European philosophers. The future must have looked
bright indeed for Heidegger in 1930, despite the increasing political turmoil in Germany.

The Hitler Era

The year 1933 was one of the darkest of the twentieth century, and
was surely Heidegger's darkest year as well, since it tarnished his
reputation for eternity. It was the year of Hitler's rise to power. Far
from opposing Hitler or considering exile, Heidegger offered his
talents to the new regime as rector of the University of Freiburg (a
position similar in American terms to provost or vice president of
academic affairs). Heidegger officially joined the Nazi Party in
May, and later that month gave his infamous rectoral address,
"The Self-Assertion of the German University"—a legitimate
philosophical work accompanied bizarrely by Nazi march music
and the one-armed Fascist salute. Far worse documents from this
period have been published, including letters from Heidegger ending with an enthusiastic "Sieg Heil" for the "Führer." Heidegger's
motives for supporting the Nazis remain a matter of controversy,
as do the depth and duration of his support for the Hitler movement. Although Heidegger heaped scorn on the crude racist
Nazism of hack philosophers like Alfred Rosenberg, the record
shows that he denounced one colleague as a pacifist and another as
the friend of a Jew. Further controversy surrounds Heidegger's
failure to attend the funeral of Husserl, who died in 1938; nor did
he do much to ease the dangerous situation of Elisabeth
Blochmann, another Jewish friend and likely mistress (their letters
are clear enough for me, at least). The firing of Karl Jaspers at
Heidelberg was greeted by Heidegger with icy silence. While the
debate over Heidegger and Nazism will surely continue, few

would deny that the Hitler period places the philosopher in a rather ugly light.

The rectorate ended in just one year, as Heidegger grew disillusioned with the failure of his reform proposals and his waning influence in national academic circles. The philosopher retreated into the shell of family life, which was expanded in 1935 to include foster daughter Erika Birle (1921–), an ethnic German orphan from São Paulo, Brazil. As World War II approached, Heidegger's lecture courses focused increasingly on Germany's great intellectual past. During the war itself, he continued his lectures in Freiburg, although the city was eventually decimated by an Allied bombing raid. In 1944, as the German war effort approached final collapse, Heidegger was drafted into the *Volkssturm* or People's Militia, though he mainly did guard duty and saw no actual combat. With Freiburg increasingly in danger, Heidegger began to deliver his manuscripts to his brother Fritz in Messkirch for safekeeping. Their hometown was unexpectedly struck by a bombing raid of its own on February 22, 1945, but Heidegger's manuscripts escaped destruction.

Life after WWII

For Heidegger, as for the German nation, the end of the war brought significant trauma, but also a chance for renewal. Heidegger's homeland lay in ruins, as did his reputation. His sons Jörg and Hermann were held by the Soviet Army as prisoners of war, and would remain so for years to come, as Stalin used the labor power of captured Germans to rebuild his country. Heidegger was also stripped of his right to teach. For some reason he had counted on his former friend Jaspers to say good things on his behalf, but Jaspers actually sent the Denazification Commission a damning assessment of Heidegger's character and philosophy. For some time there was even talk of punishing Heidegger further by confiscating his personal library to help restock the University of Münster, although this disaster was avoided. The philosopher must have felt like a caged animal. As the pressure mounted, he sought psychiatric help. He also approached his old mentor the Archbishop Gröber for the first time in years, making an abject and tearful apology for his misdeeds.

Even so, a new window of opportunity opened for Heidegger at this time: a window facing France, the very nation whose soldiers now occupied Freiburg. Jean-Paul Sartre, already the intellectual lion of Paris, had made ingenious use of the ideas of Husserl and Heidegger in his own major work *Being and Nothingness* (1943). Although Heidegger's opinion of Sartre as a philosopher sank from initial enthusiasm to eventual rejection, he owes Sartre a great debt for spreading his ideas in increasingly serious circles abroad. But it is perhaps Jean Beaufret who deserves the most credit for Heidegger's great influence in France, which continues to this day. Following the war, Beaufret used his contacts in the French military to deliver an admiring letter to Heidegger. In 1946, the two men met for the first time, beginning a close association most famous for the public "Letter on Humanism," addressed by Heidegger to Beaufret and containing criticisms of Sartre and existentialism. It was also Beaufret who arranged for Heidegger to make a number of trips to France, on which the philosopher met such figures as the poet René Char and the Cubist painter Georges Braque. Unfortunately, Heidegger did not always repay Beaufret's efforts with kindness, sometimes treating him in arrogant or dismissive fashion.

Another window of opportunity pointed to the North: in the surprising direction of Bremen, the northern German city most famous for the folktale legend of its animal musicians. Bremen was generally regarded as a city of merchants rather than intellectuals, and had no university at the time. Yet fate would bring Heidegger and Bremen together—giving Heidegger a second grand entrance into philosophy, and turning Bremen into one of the secret capitals of twentieth-century thought. Heidegger's former student, the cultural historian Heinrich Wiegand Petzet, used family connections to arrange for Heidegger to give a series of lectures to the Bremen Club in 1949. The audience, made up largely of shippers and industrialists with little academic training, listened patiently as Heidegger read some of the most seductive and bizarre pages of twentieth-century philosophy, in a set of lectures called *Insight Into What Is*. These lectures introduce the dominant themes of the so-called later period of Heidegger's career: the question concerning technology, the independence of things from human perception, and above all the mysterious "fourfold" of earth, sky, gods, and mortals, which has baffled Heidegger's readers ever since.

Much of Heidegger's work of the 1950s amounts to spin-off essays from this series of Bremen lectures, which have not yet been fully translated into English.

In 1951, Heidegger was permitted to resume lecturing at the University of Freiburg, though he did so less regularly than before. Jaspers and Arendt also reappeared in his life, with mixed results: while the wounds between Heidegger and Jaspers never fully healed, Arendt became Heidegger's right-hand woman in the United States, finding publication deals and competent translators for his work.

The 1960s found Heidegger an old man, though further interesting events did occur in his life. He made a first trip to his beloved Greece in 1962. He engaged in a dispute with the philosopher Ernst Tugendhat, and endured a lengthy attack from the Leftist thinker Theodor Adorno. He also began a troubled friendship with the famous poet Paul Celan, a Romanian Jew who had lost his family during the war and eventually committed suicide. Heidegger also granted a secret 1966 interview to the German magazine *Der Spiegel*, on condition that it remain unpublished until the philosopher's death. Heidegger lived long enough to witness the passing of many of his old friends. Karl Jaspers died in 1969. Hannah Arendt, once the brilliant young woman of Marburg, died before Heidegger in 1975 after a distinguished career in America. Heidegger himself died on May 26, 1976, of an uncertain ailment. He is buried in his hometown of Messkirch, where his tombstone is marked with a stylized star, a notable contrast with the Christian crosses on the neighboring graves of his family.

Appearance and Character

In physical terms, Heidegger was a small man with a dark complexion and striking eyes. He had uncommon athletic ability for a thinker, and was especially adept at skiing. His voice could be thin and high-pitched, as can be heard in several available recordings, yet many found it hypnotic nonetheless. Heidegger's style of dress was often unusual for academic gatherings, with a wardrobe featuring ski suits and peasant costumes as regular items. As a teacher, he worked rare magic on his students through his avoidance of dull academic jargon and his ability to bring the great thinkers of the past to life. Yet he could also be a bully: intimidating gifted students such as Gadamer into prolonged years of self-doubt, snapping at his French admirers for their ignorance well into his elderly years, or rewarding his loyal admirer Petzet with belittling remarks and at least one humiliating prank. Heidegger's writing style is powerful, if somewhat repetitive. His letters show a great deal of thoughtfulness accompanied by flashes of sarcasm and anger, especially in the frustrating early stages of his career. Although Heidegger traveled relatively little by the standards of his era, he seems to have been affected deeply by those few journeys that he did take, especially in the cases of southern France and the Greek island of Delos. Finally, Heidegger is tainted by political scandal to a greater degree than any comparable figure of Western intellectual history. This complicated personality is rated by many, including me, as the greatest philosopher of the past century.

2

A Radical Phenomenologist

Many interpreters of Heidegger like to split his career into "early" and "late" periods, with various competing theories as to when the turn in his thinking occurred. There are understandable reasons for this procedure: clear differences in terminology and tone are found in various phases of Heidegger's career. Even so, it is largely fruitless to read Heidegger as split into two distinct periods. His philosophy is a unified organism from its first appearance in 1919 to its final fruits in the early 1960s. When speaking of a maple tree, no one speaks of "early" and "late" tree, but simply tells the story of the birth, growth, and death of the single tree. It would be equally pointless when reading a novel to speak of a turn between "early" and "late" *War and Peace*: instead, we simply recount the plot of the novel and the often-surprising fate of its major characters.

Yet I would also not want to take the opposite approach, and write a book on Heidegger that split his thinking into such topics as "Heidegger's theory of knowledge," "Heidegger's philosophy of art," and "Heidegger's political philosophy." Why not? In the first place, we should take seriously Heidegger's view that every great thinker has only *one* great thought, rather than numerous separate ideas that could be classified under familiar headings. But even more important is the fact that a philosophy cannot be reduced to its *content*. A philosophy is not a set of definite opinions about specific subjects, one that would change completely with each minor change in the author's views. If your best friend swings overnight from atheism to religious zealotry, he still remains the same person; his personality and style of argument will remain the same even when his opinions have diametrically shifted. France was monarchist in 1782 and revolutionary in 1792, yet displayed the same French sensuality and intellectualism after the great event as before. The same holds for a great philosophy, even when its specific doctrines change over time. To explain a philosophy is not to explain the content of the philosopher's opinions at any given moment. Instead, to explain a philosophy means to approach the central insight that guides it through its entire lifespan, through all surface changes of opinion and all troubled reversals of viewpoint.

A philosophy is a living organism. Like every organism, it is born when it separates from its parents. Initially fragile and dependent on ancestors, a philosophy grows by expanding its core insight in surprising directions, by grafting ideas from other philosophies, and finally by asserting independence (sometimes violently) from its parents. The current fashion among scholars is to exaggerate the link between Heidegger and Aristotle, a philosopher with whom he has relatively little in common. Heidegger's true intellectual father is a far more obvious candidate: his teacher Edmund Husserl. Without Husserl, no Heidegger; without phenomenology, no *Being and Time*. It is Husserl who taught Heidegger how to use his own eyes, and Heidegger's various declarations of independence are aimed explicitly at Husserl, who was both as nurturing and as suffocating as mentors always are. The birth of Heidegger as an original philosopher comes in 1919, at the age of twenty-nine. Although traces of Husserl's DNA are still visible at this stage, the Heideggerian philosophy in 1919 is already an independent organism.

Heidegger is best understood as a heretic among the phenomenologists, just as Spinoza's philosophy can be seen as a Cartesian heresy, Hegel's philosophy as a Kantian heresy, Buddhism as a Hindu heresy, and the United States as a British heresy. Before turning to the heretic, we should briefly discuss the mentor whose work he radicalized: Edmund Husserl. This will require another biographical detour, though a shorter one than the last.

Husserl's Phenomenology

Edmund Husserl was born to Jewish parents on April 8, 1859, in Prossnitz in Moravia (now in the Czech Republic, but then part of the Austro-Hungarian Empire). Following secondary school in Olmütz, he attended the universities of Leipzig, Berlin, and Vienna. His initial focus was on mathematics, a field in which he flourished under such well-known teachers as Weierstrass and Kronecker. He received his doctorate in mathematics in Vienna in 1882, with a dissertation entitled "Contributions to the Theory of the Calculus of Variations."

BRENTANO AND INTENTIONALITY

Fate, however, had a different vocation in store for Husserl than mathematics. In 1883 he came under the spell of the charismatic philosopher Franz Brentano, the same Catholic rebel who would later captivate the young Heidegger and the young Sigmund Freud as well. Brentano's classic book, *Psychology from the Empirical Standpoint*, can be seen as a forerunner of Husserl's phenomenology. At this time philosophy seemed to be steadily losing ground to the booming natural sciences. In response to this situation, Brentano tried to carve out a special domain for philosophy by sharply distinguishing between mental acts and physical reality. Unlike the physical world, everything mental is distinguished by "intentionality" (an old medieval term revived by Brentano), which means that every mental act is directed toward an object. At each moment I see something, laugh at something, worry about something, or scream at something. All mental acts contain other objects: this "intentional inexistence," as Brentano calls it, creates a radical break between the physical and mental realms.

Under Brentano's influence, Husserl had discovered that philosophy was his true calling. Yet their relations were not always pleasant. Despite his rigorous mathematical training, Husserl was a sensitive and intuitive young man who often despaired when the master logician Brentano would smash his vague new insights with a single blow. For this reason, he must have felt somewhat relieved when Brentano sent him to the University of Halle to do his *Habilitation* in philosophy with Professor Carl Stumpf. In the same year Husserl converted to the Lutheran faith (at least officially), and in the following year he was married. Husserl and Stumpf formed an excellent relationship. Husserl's *Habilitation* thesis was on the concept of number, leading in 1891 to the publication of his first book, *The Philosophy of Arithmetic*. Even at this stage, Husserl dreamed of a new universal foundation for philosophy, one that would render all previous philosophies obsolete.

DISCOURAGEMENT AND THE BIRTH OF PHENOMENOLOGY

From 1887 to 1901, Husserl struggled as an instructor in Halle. He was frequently discouraged and insecure, and considered abandoning philosophy entirely. This long and difficult period ended with the bombshell publication in 1900–1901 of the multivolume work *Logical Investigations*. This book was one of the greatest achievements in all of recent philosophy, and provided endless fascination to Heidegger during his student years. It also marked the birth of the name "phenomenology" for Husserl's thinking, a name that would echo throughout the world in the decades to come. The first volume of *Logical Investigations* is an attack on "psychologism": the theory that logical laws are really just psychological laws of the human mind, a popular view at the time. The remainder of the work contains Husserl's trailblazing theories of linguistic and nonlinguistic signs, a new theory of wholes and parts, and above all, a new model of intentionality that departed from Brentano's in significant respects.

Among other differences, Brentano held that all intentionality is a kind of representation: a presence of something before the human mind. Husserl modified this to say that every intention is an *objectifying* act, including not just theoretical awareness, but also such obscure intentions as wishes, fears, confusion, and anger, all of which Husserl places on equal footing with conscious theoretical observation. Even more importantly, Husserl noticed that intentional objects are never fully present, since they always show us only one profile (or "adumbration") while hiding numerous others. In other words, a tree or house is never completely present to us, but is only a principle that unifies all our various perceptions of the tree and house from many different angles and distances. Both of these breakthroughs were later pushed further by Heidegger: Husserl's new interest in vague and obscure forms of intentionality was transformed into Heidegger's theory of moods, while the permanent invisibility of intentional objects would be radicalized into Heidegger's revolutionary analysis of tools.

SUCCESS

Although the *Logical Investigations* needed time to gain their full influence, the importance of the book was immediately recognized by the mathematician David Hilbert of the University of Göttingen. Hilbert urged that Husserl receive an assistant professorship in Göttingen. In 1901, Husserl received and accepted the call; the dark days of Halle had come to an end. The Göttingen years were surely the happiest period of Husserl's life. He had become the center of a worldwide philosophical movement, and would soon become the editor of a journal devoted entirely to his own style of philosophy. He basked in the admiration of his students, even while encouraging them to reject the authority of Husserl or anyone else and accept only what they could see directly with their own eyes. In later years Husserl was often criticized for delivering long-winded monologues in the classroom, but in the Göttingen period he seems to have been a good listener and an open-minded conversation partner. He also drastically reworked his philosophy in a way that Heidegger and other younger admirers would eventually reject. Stated briefly, Husserl turned toward the brand of philosophy known as idealism—placing emphasis on human consciousness rather than on the world itself. This turn is most clearly expressed in his 1913 book *Ideas for a Pure Phenomenology and a Phenomenological Philosophy*, usually called *Ideas I*, since two additional volumes were published after Husserl's death.

In 1916, as we have seen, Husserl was called to Freiburg as full professor, and remained in that city even after his retirement. Although Husserl graciously published Heidegger's *Being and Time* in his journal, he was somewhat disappointed with his former student's book, as can be seen from critical handwritten notes found in his personal copy. It seemed to him that Heidegger had relapsed from philosophy into anthropology, given Heidegger's detailed focus in the book on human existence. In 1929, Husserl's students and friends produced a so-called *Festschrift* for his seventieth birthday—following the German tradition of publishing collected essays by various authors in honor of a respected figure. Heidegger was given the honor of presenting the work to Husserl, yet the personal and philosophical distance between them continued to grow.

HUSSERL'S LATE CAREER

The rise of the Nazis in 1933 ended Husserl's central role at the University of Freiburg, as Jewish faculty members were persecuted. Yet Husserl continued to work intensely on philosophy, discussing new ideas with his talented disciple Eugen Fink, and honored by the continued pilgrimage of foreign admirers wishing to meet him. In 1935 Austria was not yet under Nazi rule, and Husserl accepted a lecture invitation to Vienna, the city where he had learned philosophy from Brentano a half-century earlier. Later that year, he enjoyed great success with further lectures in Prague, another city just a few years from Nazi invasion. These lectures contained the germ of his final great work: *The Crisis of the European Sciences and Transcendental Phenomenology*, whose first pages appeared in 1936. The final year of Husserl's life was dominated by a struggle with illness, and he died in Freiburg on April 27, 1938. Heidegger's failure to attend his former teacher's funeral under Nazi rule is viewed by his critics as an act of supreme cowardice. Heidegger explained it as simply a human failing, and sometimes claimed to have been sick in bed.

Like all great mentors, Husserl provided Heidegger with a brilliant model of how to reach his own mode of thinking. Yet great teachers can take years to overcome, and often provoke violent reactions in students as they struggle to see the world with their own eyes. The Martin Heidegger of 1919, not yet thirty years old, must have felt a strange mixture of thrill and anxiety as he presented his own first breakthroughs in philosophy, which already show decisive and permanent ruptures with Husserl.

1919: Heidegger's Breakthrough

As the Central Powers collapsed at the end of World War I, revolution swept through the streets of Germany. Everywhere there was talk of reform, of the need to reconstruct the whole of society and the university based on some guiding principle. The young Heidegger also had revolutionary tendencies, though not yet in the service of any political movement. In his lecture courses of 1919, he begins by addressing the widespread calls for reform. The title of these lectures in English is *Towards the Definition of Philosophy*, though *On the Vocation of Philosophy* is another possible translation.

REFORMING SOCIETY THROUGH SCIENCE

In Heidegger's view, the task of philosophy is not to provide a new world-view for the public. A new world-view is always superficial and arbitrary, lacking deep roots, and so would not be able to save society. By contrast, Heidegger says that true reform is possible only through *science*. It should be noted that in German, the word for science (*Wissenschaft*) is not restricted to the exact natural sciences, as is usually the case in English. Instead, it refers to any kind of systematic knowledge at all. In the German sense of the term, history, sociology, and literary theory are also sciences; numerous German philosophers have used the word "science" to describe what they do. In fact, the young Heidegger insists that philosophy is the primordial science, the one with the broadest and deepest roots of all. The fundamental knowledge that we seek cannot come from any *particular* science: for example, we cannot reform the whole of society based on discoveries in psychology. After all, psychology is a limited field that cannot take account of equally useful insights drawn from physics, history, engineering, or aesthetics. Only philosophy has no limit to the objects it can discuss, and this means that only philosophy can provide a radical new basis for society. But philosophy is something we learn only by doing it ourselves, since the *history* of philosophy cannot help us: unless we are thinking for ourselves, we can learn nothing from Plato or Kant except superficial information about their opinions. Only those who deal with the deep and radical problems of philosophy for themselves can learn anything from the great philosophers of the past.

BEYOND HUSSERL

In 1919, the best example of a radical philosopher seeing the world with his own eyes seemed to be Edmund Husserl, Heidegger's own teacher. During this period, Heidegger still believes that phenomenology is the only way to reconstruct our entire model of the world. Yet a surprising twist to Heidegger's loyalties has already begun to emerge. In his 1919 lectures, the young Heidegger begins to imply that Husserl has not seen the world radically enough—that there are still damaging biases that haunt phenomenology. Although still praising his teacher, Heidegger begins to make subtle remarks about the need to reform phenomenology itself.

When we want to say in English that something exists, we say "there is" or "there are" such things. There are submarines. There are tornadoes. There are islands, jungles, and even fictional characters. In German they say *es gibt*, which literally means "it gives." The young Heidegger now asks what "it gives" means, a question he had been asking even in his doctoral thesis six years earlier. He is not interested in making clever grammatical jokes about the mysterious "it" that supposedly "gives." Instead, he simply wants to know what it really means when we say that a thing is. What sort of reality do things have? For Husserl, who walled philosophy off from the natural sciences, the reality of a thing is to appear as a phenomenon for human consciousness; any existence of things outside consciousness is secondary. In 1919, Heidegger begins to radicalize phenomenology, turning it into something completely different. For Heidegger as he reaches maturity, unlike for Husserl, if we say "there is a city called Beirut," this cannot mean that Beirut exists as a series of appearances in consciousness. In the young Heidegger's terminology, Beirut is neither a physical occurrence nor an appearance in consciousness. Instead, Beirut is an independent *event*. All things that exist have the character of events.

EQUIPMENT

At this point, Heidegger offers an example that is both brilliant and, by contemporary standards, somewhat offensive. As he stands in a lecture hall in Freiburg, addressing his students from the podium, Heidegger notes that professor and students all use the various objects in the room, taking them for granted. The podium is simply used, not consciously seen. The desks of the students, their pens and notebooks, are also taken for granted as useful items before they are ever clearly and consciously noticed. Heidegger now asks us to imagine what would happen if a "Senegal Negro" suddenly entered the room. This unlucky foreigner might have no concept at all of a lecture hall and its usual equipment. He might be utterly confused by the podium and have no idea of how to use it. Even so, he would not see the podium and the desks as meaningless colors and shapes. Instead, he might think of the podium as an item for voodoo or witchcraft, or as a barrier for hiding from arrows and slingstones. The "Senegal Negro's" failure to understand the room does not mean that the room is a sheer perception without any practical use. Instead, he would encounter the room as a form of "equipmental strangeness."

This is what the world means for the young Heidegger: it is not a spectacle of colors and shapes, but rather an environment in which all things have a special significance for us and are linked with one another in a specific way. What we learn from the visitor from Senegal is that objects always have a highly specific meaning even when they are not lucidly present in consciousness. Things are events, not perceptual or physical occurrences. They are a "how," not a "what"—in other words, they cannot be reduced to a list of traits and qualities that might be found in a dictionary. To repeat, the things encountered by humans are events, and this means that there is more to them than anything we can see or say about them. If I look at a flower from thousands of different angles and perform hundreds of experiments on it, all of these actions will never add up to the total reality of the flower, which is always something deeper than whatever we might see, no matter how hard we work. In some way phenomenology misses this point, since it claims that the true being of a thing lies in the way it is present in our minds. Under the influence of the German philosopher Wilhelm Dilthey (1833–1911), Heidegger realized that historical reality is a deeper and darker layer of the world than Husserl's philosophy of phenomena can grasp. History tries to come to grips with events that are often complex and murky, not lucid appearances for human consciousness.

THE PROBLEM WITH SCIENCE

For the young Heidegger, then, the true reality of things is not visible, but hides from conscious view. In order to gain knowledge of things, any science has to objectify them, and to objectify things means to "de-live" them. In other words, knowledge always cuts things down to size or turns them into caricatures through some sort of oversimplification. No theory of numbers, birds, chemicals, or Stone Age societies will ever be able to exhaust the reality of these topics. To treat them scientifically means to "cut them off at the knees," converting them from mysterious and multifaceted things into concepts whose basic features can be clearly listed in a glossary. While this distortion is inevitable, it is a distortion nonetheless. Scientific knowledge of any kind, including Husserl's brand of philosophy, always fails to do justice to the things in the world, which are dark and stormy events locked in a network with other such events, rather than crystal-clear sets of knowable properties. To some extent, scientific knowledge is always a waltz with illusions, or at least with exaggerations.

We have seen that Husserl tried to save philosophy by criticizing scientific naturalism. For Husserl the world is not made primarily of forces, chemicals, potential and kinetic energy, or electromagnetic fields. What comes first for him is always phenomena perceived by humans, since these provide the true basis for any scientific theory. The young Heidegger now risks a bold criticism of his teacher. According to Heidegger, the problem is not the dominance of naturalism, but the dominance of *theory*. If scientific theories fail to do justice to the things, phenomenology also fails. If science wrongly reduces the mysterious things of the world to pieces of physical mass, phenomenology wrongly reduces them to appearances in consciousness. What things really are is events.

1920–21: Facticity and Time

A few semesters later, we find Heidegger pursuing his old religious interests, lecturing on such key Christian figures as St. Paul and St. Augustine. This lecture course is available in English as *The Phenomenology of Religious Life*, and is highly recommended to anyone interested in the themes it covers. Here we need only focus on Heidegger's development of the new philosophical concepts that make his historical writings possible.

PHILOSOPHY REDEFINES ITSELF CONSTANTLY

Earlier, Heidegger claimed that all the specific sciences are too limited in the objects they describe; by contrast, philosophy has a universal scope. In 1920–21, he adds a new observation about the difference between philosophy and science. Namely, only philosophy constantly seeks to redefine itself and redetermine its own meaning. While each of the sciences goes through an occasional state of crisis that forces it to reconsider its basic concepts, such as physics after the development of relativity and the quantum theory, for philosophy this must happen constantly. Indeed, philosophy is nothing but a perpetual crisis and new beginning. All specific sciences begin by presupposing the nature of their object: only in moments of especial turmoil does chemistry ask what a chemical is or geometry ask what a shape is. It is philosophy alone that constantly faces crisis by redefining its subject matter again and again.

FACTICITY

Not only would Husserl agree with all of this, he actually said it all before Heidegger did. But there is something further that Husserl did not already notice. Pushing his earlier criticisms still further, Heidegger insists that philosophy cannot look at reality from the outside, by way of its appearance. To understand human activity, we have to view it as an independent event, not as something looked at by an observer. To use a German word, we have to view it as *Vollzug*, which means performance or execution, not one of Husserl's major terms. Human life is not something visible from the outside, but must be seen in the very act, performance, or execution of its own reality, which always exceeds any of the properties that we can list about it. In other words, life is "factical," and is marked by what Heidegger calls "facticity." The facticity of life simply means that life cannot be adequately described in theoretical terms. Human life is always immersed in a specific situation, involved with its surroundings in a very particular way. This facticity always remains partly obscure, and for this reason human life cannot be approached by the methods used in the sciences to describe inanimate matter.

Heidegger's name for human existence is Dasein ("being there" or simply "existence"), a word almost always left in the original German. For Heidegger in 1920–21, factical Dasein is the only subject matter of philosophy, for two related reasons. First, the only way to avoid reducing things to their appearance is to focus on the facticity of human life in its environment, where everything has a tacit meaning or function before we consciously notice it. Second, philosophy only arises out of a factical situation in the first place: Plato, Descartes, and Hegel were not disembodied souls floating through empty space, but were real human beings who only began to philosophize in a specific historical setting.

ENVIRONMENT

Husserl was right to say that we should abandon all traditional philosophical theories and see things with our own eyes. However, for Heidegger what we see with those eyes is not objects made up of visible properties, but an environment, and our environment is partly determined by history. In the environment, all objects gain their meaning only in their relations with one another. Everything belongs to a total system of meaning: for example, individual car parts might seem meaningless or useless in isolation, but when inserted in the car they immediately regain their full significance. While this is obviously true for objects such as cars and lecture podiums, it is equally true for my dealings with other humans and even with myself. I do not usually encounter other people as *homo sapiens*, nor do I simply observe isolated moods in my own mind. Instead, all of these things are interpreted according to their significance with respect to other things in the world. With this method of turning toward factical human life, Heidegger aims to do nothing less than revolutionize all of philosophy. The traditional categories of philosophy, found in Plato and Aristotle and later thinkers, are nothing but external descriptions of the properties of things. Any normal categories we use to describe things will fail to capture them as real events in their performance or execution. For this reason, we need an entirely new set of categories to do justice to factical Dasein.

THE IMPORTANCE OF TIME

To do justice to human Dasein, we need to interpret it in terms of *time*. Heidegger urges that time should not be viewed externally as an "occurrence." In other words, time cannot be understood when it is measured by clocks, stopwatches, or calendars, since all of these instruments distort time in the same way that science distorts its objects, by viewing them from the outside. What we need to do is find some way to grasp time as an event—in its execution, performance, or facticity. Although Husserl also wrote a famous work on time-consciousness (edited by Martin Heidegger himself) Husserl is still talking about the *consciousness* of time, not time itself. Heidegger's central misgiving about phenomenology is the way it treats various topics in terms of how they appear to consciousness, since this gives us only an external or superficial access to things. Whereas Husserl might have beautifully analyzed our consciousness of podiums and desks in the lecture hall, Heidegger tried to show what these things are for us before all explicit consciousness. The same is true of time. Heidegger wants to discuss not the consciousness of time, but its facticity—the ambiguous way that time is already at work in our environment before we have noticed it at all.

TWO KINDS OF THEORIZING

But if talking about something always means to distort or kill it, how is philosophy possible? After all, we have to say something about any subject, unless we wish to sit in silence. According to Heidegger, the proper way to describe anything in its factical reality is through what he calls "formal indication." Although Husserl never uses this concept, Heidegger boldly calls it the hidden meaning of phenomenology.

For Husserl, there are two ways to theorize about phenomena: "generalization" and "formalization." The difference between them is easy to explain. Generalization is the kind of theorizing that describes the properties of things, and it always moves step by step in a series of levels. For example, I might say that this cactus is green, this green is a color, this color is a sensory phenomenon, and this sensory phenomenon is a reality. In short, we are dealing here with what traditional philosophy called the "essence" of a thing.

Formalization is different. It does not need to move step by step, but can be done at any level of the process. For instance, I can say that this cactus *is,* but just as easily say that this green *is* or this color *is.* Here, we are dealing with what traditional philosophy called the "existence" of a thing. Not surprisingly, Heidegger rejects both generalization and formalization as models of theoretical awareness, since both of them reduce things to their external properties rather than grasping them in their deeper factical reality. "Formal indication" is Heidegger's name for the new kind of theorizing that somehow points to the facticity of life without reducing it to a set of surface qualities.

FORMAL INDICATION

Instead of listing all the adjectives that describe a cactus, or informing us of the obvious fact that the cactus "is," formal indication is a kind of knowledge that hints at some deeper reality of the cactus without ever claiming to exhaust it. In a certain sense, the whole of Heidegger's career amounts to nothing but variations on this same theme. For Heidegger, philosophy is a way of making things present without making them present. It does this by means of suggestions, hints, or allusions to the being of things that lies deeper than their presence to our consciousness.

Philosophy, Heidegger insists, is not a theoretical science. With this statement, he claims to cut against the grain of the entire history of philosophy, which overlooks the execution or performance of things in favor of their outward appearance. The thirty-one-year-old Heidegger no longer sees himself as just a good phenomenologist carrying Husserl's banner a bit further. On the contrary: he already sees himself as the key figure in the entire history of philosophy. In Heidegger's own mind, it is he alone who liberates factical life from the traditional categories that oppress it.

1921–22: The Triple Structure of Life

Heidegger's 1921–22 lecture course is entitled *Phenomenological Interpretations of Aristotle*—one of his many courses with misleading titles. In the printed version of the lectures, Heidegger actually spends less than a dozen pages discussing Aristotle before changing the subject. As he explains it, we cannot write the history of philosophy without philosophizing ourselves; hence, we must turn from Aristotle back to factical life. But life does not exist alone in a vacuum and later come down into a world. Instead, life and its environment are inseparable from the start. Dasein is never an isolated human creature, but always inhabits a specific environment made up of other things and humans. Life is always *this* particular life and no other or, as Heidegger puts it, life is "thisly"—a term that Heidegger seems to borrow from the medieval philosophy of Duns Scotus.

Life always has a threefold structure of past, future, and present. At any given moment, life does not choose the state in which it finds itself. There is no erasing our current situation, no matter how glorious or miserable it may be; our current life is already there before us, as the hand we are forced to play. The most we can do is try to work with the situation as we find it—and every moment, no matter how dull or horrible, has its possibilities. This is the threefold structure of life, which Heidegger sees as a truer form of temporality than clock time. We find ourselves delivered to a situation that must be dealt with somehow (past). Yet we are not mere slaves to this situation, since we go to work on our current situation by glimpsing possibilities in it that we can try to actualize (future). Finally, every moment of factical life is a profound tension between what is given to us and how we confront it (present). Life is a kind of *unrest*, forever torn between two poles of reality. Life is movement, or "motility."

OBJECTS AND THINGS

Heidegger emphasizes that the categories of life are drawn from life itself, not projected onto life by an outside observer. The motives for the philosophy of life always swell up from within the very heart of life. No scientist or philosopher can stand outside of life, uncontaminated by its ambiguous threefold structure. We must avoid any sort of theory that converts things into nothing but visible "objects," since this only strips away the full reality of things and reduces them to caricatures. Things are not objects: instead, they have significance, which means that they belong to a system of relations with other things in the environment. We encounter everything only from in the midst of life. To view things as part of "nature" is secondary to how we usually encounter them in everyday life, as Husserl already knew. But whereas Husserl thought that our encounter with things means viewing them as phenomena in consciousness, Heidegger thinks we encounter things mostly by taking them for granted.

Just as factical human life "temporalizes," torn in two directions between the situation it discovers and the possibilities that it projects onto this situation, the same can be said of the things we encounter. If someone has given me a gun, then this has already happened and there is no way to change it (past). Yet it remains my own decision whether to interpret the gun as something to be thrown in the garbage, sold, donated to a museum, melted down, hidden under the bed for self-defense, or used in a murder or bank robbery (future). The qualities of things emerge within factical life itself, and are not just external properties of those things. Even more generally, things have meaning only because human Dasein has the structure of *care*. This means that human beings always take a stand within the world, occupied with it, fascinated by it, overjoyed or horrified by it. We do not primarily look at the world like neutral observers, but care about what happens in it.

TRIOS OF TERMS

Heidegger's writings are filled with many different triads of terms, some more clearly explained than others. To cite an example from later in his career, Heidegger claims in *Being and Time* that every question has three parts: (1) that which is asked about, (2) that which is interrogated, (3) and that which is to be found out by the asking. Read in isolation, this hairsplitting analysis can seem either impressively subtle or annoying and arbitrary. The secret to unlocking all these triple structures is to realize that they are all variants of the same underlying concept: temporality. In every one of Heidegger's trios of terms, something is given ahead of time, some specific attitude is taken toward what is given, and the intersection of these two poles gives us the shadowy and ambiguous present.

Of all the threefolds in Heidegger's career, the one from the 1921–22 course is the murkiest of them all, and is explained in some of the worst prose of Heidegger's life. He first speaks of a difference between inclination, distance, and sequestration; this confusing triad is paralleled by the related threesome of "relucence," "ruinance," and "larvance" (all of them invented by Heidegger himself). Since this strange terminology does not survive into Heidegger's mature period, it can safely be forgotten.

RUINANCE

But while none of these terms are retained by Heidegger, he does give a detailed discussion of *ruinance*, and draws several interesting consequences. Factical Dasein (a.k.a. human life) is always in an environment in which it is tempted, seduced, soothed, or estranged. Whereas Husserl thinks that human life is primarily conscious awareness, or "intentionality," the increasingly rebellious Heidegger asks his students with open sarcasm: "Did intentionality fall from the sky?" This is just another way of insisting that human life always belongs to a specific environment. Against what Husserl says, philosophy cannot be free of presuppositions, since this would result only in an empty, external description of the world. Philosophy must *always* have presuppositions, because philosophy itself arises from the ruinance of factical life, just as poetry, engineering, or commerce do. Philosophy, says Heidegger, should be a *countermovement* to ruinance. We never rise above our environment to some pure, lofty pedestal and pass judgment on the world, as if we were untainted by it. What we can do is liberate the hidden presuppositions of life even while living it, making those suppositions partly visible by interpreting them.

KAIROLOGICAL TIME

Returning to his earlier fascination with the New Testament, Heidegger invokes the Greek word *kairos*. The Greek language has two words for time: *kairos* and *chronos*. Chronological time is the kind measured objectively in days and minutes, which Heidegger wants to reject as a way of understanding the time of factical Dasein. By contrast, *kairological* time refers to the richness of one special moment, and thus fits much better with the sort of philosophy that Heidegger is trying to develop. The time of Dasein is not about minutes passing on a clock, but about the tense interplay between two opposite poles of the world: the ruinance of our fascination with the environment, and the countermovement that frees us from our surroundings without ever freeing us entirely. Ironically, it is ruinance that hides *kairos* from us, clouding the real situation of our temporality and seducing us into thinking that time means days on a calendar. It is also ruinance that leads us to interpret our moods in terms of psychology: torment, agony, and confusion are wrongly viewed as subjective feelings unfolding inside of consciousness. In fact, they are not just feelings, but ways in which the depth of our factical reality shows itself.

NOTHINGNESS

In closing, it should be noted that Heidegger mentions *nothingness* here, a theme that eventually becomes highly important for him. If factical human life can be viewed as a kind of collapse, onto what does it collapse? On what floor or bedrock does it come crashing down? The surprising answer is "nothingness." Since factical life always has a highly specific character, it is finite, not unlimited. What lies beyond this finitude of our lives is nothingness— not the *concept* of nothingness or negation, but a genuine nothingness in reality itself. This topic will return a bit later.

1923: Being in the Public World

The 1923 lecture course turned out to be the last in Heidegger's early Freiburg period before he accepted his new position in Marburg. The title is *Ontology: Hermeneutics of Facticity*. Like many of Heidegger's better titles, this one summarizes the whole of his philosophical position at this point in his career. Ontology is the branch of philosophy that deals with the basic structure of being, and by 1923 Heidegger was already well on his way to becoming the great philosopher of being. But as we already know, being cannot be viewed from the outside by means of traditional descriptive categories. Being must be seen in its facticity as a shadowy event, not a lucid visible spectacle. Finally, the way to unlock this facticity is not through scientific theory, but through *hermeneutics*—a term derived from the Greek word for interpretation. Reality always partly eludes our grasp; it is not directly seen, but always interpreted in a specific way and from a specific standpoint. Taken as a whole, the title of this lecture course means simply that Heidegger wants to develop a theory of being through an interpretation of human life in its concrete historical reality.

HISTORICITY

This 1923 lecture course shows many of the same mixed feelings toward Husserl already encountered in earlier courses. Heidegger complains that the phenomenological movement has been ruined by superficial and wishy-washy admirers who do not fully understand it. Yet when we read Heidegger's attacks carefully, we find that they are aimed not at any of these supposed frivolous admirers, but at the theories of Edmund Husserl himself! Husserl wanted philosophy to be a "rigorous science," free of all presuppositions; by focusing only on things as they appear to us, and by analyzing these appearances in order to grasp their underlying principles, Husserl claimed to reach an "intuition of essences" of the phenomena.

Against this, Heidegger asserts that there is no philosophy without presuppositions, since all philosophy grows from a particular historical standpoint. There can be no intuition of essence, because things will always remain hidden from us to some extent. And furthermore, human beings are not solitary observers of the world, since we always belong to a specific environment that includes other people. Indeed, our access to things is not primarily through our own eyes. Before looking at things for ourselves, we have already heard about them, and we tend to interpret them in the same way as others. This is just as true of philosophy as of any other subject that interests humans. Before we select the greatest artists or musicians in human history, and before we choose our beloved person, we are already aware of how others assess them. A purely original, independent judgment is impossible.

Whereas Heidegger's earlier lecture courses said that the history of philosophy is a worthless topic unless we are philosophizing ourselves, he now stresses the other side of the issue: we cannot directly tackle philosophical problems outside of history, since these problems are already passed down to us with all sorts of historical encrustations. When we ask philosophical questions that seem original and highly personal, we do not realize that we are silently dominated by the Greek way of looking at the world. For this reason, a good deal of historical work is needed to clear up the subjects that are handed to us.

In short, Heidegger believes that phenomenology ignores history far too much. This is true not only of shallow and superficial followers of phenomenology, but even of Husserl's own way of thinking. As Heidegger puts it, we will have radical and serious phenomenology only when people see that direct presence of the world is never possible, and that concealment belongs to the very nature of phenomena. Although Heidegger does not dwell on the point, this amounts to the blunt claim that Husserl is not yet doing "radical and serious" phenomenology. Developing his own insights with increasing vigor, Heidegger has more or less announced a hostile takeover of the phenomenological movement. Since Husserl and Heidegger continued to work closely together in Freiburg, Husserl surely must have gotten wind of some of these remarks. It is a credit to Husserl's generosity and easygoing temperament that Heidegger was never excommunicated from the movement, but simply drifted away from it.

EXISTENTIALS

We have already heard Heidegger's warning that the traditional categories of philosophy do not do justice to human Dasein, which exists only as an act, event, or performance of its reality, not as something visible from the outside. Heidegger now introduces the term "existentials" for these new categories. Many of these existentials are highly memorable for those who have read Heidegger's works. Perhaps the most memorable is *das Man*, best translated as "the *they*" (just as Macquarrie and Robinson do translate it in their classic English version of *Being and Time*). We are all familiar with certain unsettling phrases in English that use "they" in an indefinite sense: "Is it really true that Professor X is being groomed as the next Dean of Humanities?" . . . "That's what they say." Here the word "they" does not refer to one person, twenty people, a 51 percent majority of people on campus, or even a 90 percent supermajority. "They" is merely an indefinite term for a loose, lazy, ambiguous, public sort of reality, for which no individual can be held responsible. We do not encounter the world directly, but always through the *talk* or *idle chatter* of the "they"—we see and say about Istanbul or the Eiffel Tower all the clichés that everyone else sees or says. This public reality is one of the existentials of human Dasein, a category of Dasein's being that can never be removed now matter how hard we try.

At all moments, Dasein has the ambiguous triple structure that we have repeatedly encountered in this chapter. Dasein is always marked by the existential structure known as "forehaving," which means that we are already in the midst of the world before saying or deciding anything about it. But Dasein is equally distinguished by the existential called "foreconception," meaning that we are not just dragged along in a stupor by the world that is given to us, but always approach it with a specific attitude toward what surrounds us. We never fully escape this interplay between the pregiven and the interpretations we make of it, which are always unified in a shadowy, two-faced present.

But although this triple structure is inescapable, Heidegger is aware that some moments of human existence come to grips with our facticity better than others. Only some instants of time are truly *moments of vision* (as Heidegger already noted with his earlier concept of kairological time). To sit and recite a list of clichés while swilling bottles of vodka and listening to advertising jingles would certainly have the same triple structure as making a brilliant political decision or discovering the theory of relativity. Nonetheless, Heidegger always tries to find ways to account for the superiority of the latter two examples. Although no human experience ever completely rises above its immersion in the public world, and although even the vodka-drinker rises above the public "they" to some small extent, Heidegger is always on the lookout for *better* ways of transcending the world: special types of boredom, special moods of anxiety, special philosophical attitudes, special moments of every kind. For us no less than for the "Senegal Negro," it often takes *strangeness* to make us more alert to everydayness, and Heidegger is among the most renowned analysts of chilling, edgy moods such as anxiety and being toward death.

SPATIALITY

To repeat an earlier point, the German word Dasein literally means being-there. The "there" where Dasein exists is called the world. Heidegger finds it useless to spend any time on the traditional problem of how our mind makes contact with a world. As Heidegger sees it, there was never any separation between them in the first place. If we speak of being-in-the-world, some people might think of this as a spatial relation, with humans inhabiting specific geometric coordinates in a grid of objective space. But never forget that these sorts of theories are precisely what Heidegger wants to avoid. We cannot define space through the modern theory that space is a set of objective coordinates filled with physical bodies. Space, like everything else, must be defined in terms of how we encounter it before any theory of space is even begun. The spatiality of the world is primarily a spatiality of *equipment*, in which everything has its own proper place and its own significance. We do not usually locate stop signs, gas stations, or traffic cones along pure axes of latitude and longitude measured from satellites, but simply notice right away if they are in the right place or wrong place with respect to other things in the environment. When they are in the wrong place, we do not respond to this by passing objective academic judgments, but simply by moving them, or perhaps by becoming frustrated or angry.

On this note, Heidegger's early Freiburg years came to an end. Barely thirty-four years old, he headed northward for a new professorship at Marburg, unaware that he would someday return to the Black Forest as Husserl's successor. Hans-Georg Gadamer gives us a picturesque anecdote about Heidegger's departure. Before leaving Freiburg, Heidegger assembled his students for a final nighttime gathering, where a bonfire was lit. He then rose to give a dramatic speech, one that began: "Be awake to the fire of

the night! The Greeks . . ." This rhetorical mixture of Greek philosophy and romantic Black Forest fire ceremony is certainly stirring. Given what would happen to Heidegger and his nation
during the 1930s, it is also somewhat ominous.

3

Marburg

Heidegger's half-decade in Marburg, from 1923–28, is one of the greatest five-year periods enjoyed by any philosopher in human history. During these years, he was forced by external pressures to write *Being and Time*, the most influential book of philosophy in the twentieth century. (Although the book belongs to the Marburg period, we will ignore it here and give it the whole of the next chapter.) It was also in Marburg that Heidegger found his mature voice as a teacher, as seen from a number of famous and beloved lecture courses: *History of the Concept of Time*, *The Basic Problems of Phenomenology*, and *The Metaphysical Foundations of Logic*. His celebrated lecture course *Plato's "Sophist"* also belongs to this period, though we cannot spare the time to discuss this massive historical work, which is loaded with citations in Greek from Plato and Aristotle.

Marburg is a charming university town perhaps ninety minutes north of Frankfurt. It is hilly enough to test one's physical endurance, and overlooks the peaceful River Lahn. The University of Marburg had already made a name for itself in the history of philosophy: it was once the employer of Christian Wolff (1679–1754), a follower of Leibniz and the first important philosopher to write in the German language. Shortly before Heidegger's arrival, it was home to the renowned "Marburg School" of neo-Kantian philosophers. No philosopher as sensitive to factical life as Heidegger could deny that a change in one's circumstances might easily spark a change in one's thinking. Settled in a new city, encountering such important new friends as Rudolf Bultmann and Hannah Arendt, and spending vacations hard at work in his distant Black Forest hut, it was in Marburg that he first began to play the Heidegger music as we know it today. While Heideggerians still make pilgrimage to Freiburg each summer, with some going so far as to build their own forest huts in imitation of the master, it would be more appropriate (and certainly more original) to build our huts near sleepy Marburg, the real capital city of Heidegger's philosophy.

1925: The Dragon Emerges

The 1925 lecture course is known misleadingly in English as *History of the Concept of Time*, and even the more complicated German title is not an accurate description of its contents. The book consists of two parts. The first is a lengthy appreciation and criticism of Husserl and the phenomenological movement. Here the criticisms of Husserl take on a new and more self-confident tone, as Heidegger feels himself on more solid footing, no longer needing to scratch and claw to break free of his teacher's influence. He even speaks with great empathy for Husserl's personal struggles in his early career, and valiantly strikes out against misreadings of his teacher. The second part of the book is essentially a lucid rehearsal of the first half of *Being and Time*. Here we will focus on the discussion of Husserl, one of the lengthiest tributes by one great philosopher to his mentor since Spinoza's book on Descartes four centuries earlier.

Heidegger's Maturity

History of the Concept of Time is the first work of Heidegger's full maturity. In the previous chapter, we saw that Heidegger had already reached his decisive breakthrough as early as 1919, at age twenty-nine. But making a breakthrough is not the same as developing it into viable form. By a "viable" idea, I mean one that is able to change the course of intellectual history even if its author is no longer there to defend it in person. If the young Heidegger had died at any time between 1919 and 1925, this would be remembered as the tragic early loss of a potential great philosopher. But if he had died immediately *after* the 1925 course, it would be remembered (assuming someone eventually published the course) as the tragic early loss of an *actual* great philosopher. Under this scenario, we would have lost *Being and Time*, the great book on Kant, the fascinating essay on artworks, the lectures on Hölderlin and Nietzsche, and all the well-known works from the later period of Heidegger's career. His star-crossed life (1889–1926) would seem eerily truncated, and we would mourn over further great works that never appeared. Yet *History of the Concept of Time* is already the polished work of a great philosopher: systematically organized, well articulated, well argued, and clearly distinguished from all the philosophies that preceded it in human history. Instead of brilliant insights half-glimpsed through swirling fog by a young thinker, we now find the thoughts of a master. We have reached a special moment in the history of recent philosophy: Husserlian phenomenology is about to be superseded by its own crown prince.

INTENTIONALITY

As Heidegger sees it, phenomenology gives us three key discoveries: (1) intentionality, (2) categorial intuition, and (3) the original sense of the *a priori*. All of these terms are much simpler than they appear, and can be explained to any reader in just a few paragraphs.

Intentionality is already familiar from earlier in the book. All consciousness is conscious *of* something. It is possible that all of the objects around me right now are illusions; nonetheless, I am still absorbed in perceiving them, whether they are really there or not. The concept of intentionality implies that we must begin with things the way they show themselves to us, without constructing theories about the world that might lie behind my conscious experience.

CATEGORIAL INTUITION

Consciousness is also defined by categorial intuition. All intentionality is highly specific, since I am always perceiving a very particular landscape with a completely determinate arrangement of things. Every element of every scene that I witness is packed with deeper layers that we were not conscious of at first. Initially, I see the green leaves of the trees, without consciously expressing that they are green, not even silently in my mind. Yet even though this green was not openly stated or acknowledged at first, it was there in the perception all along. It is not something added by me, since I found it there. We can also go further and say that we see trees

and flowers. Although the concept "and" was not immediately
obvious in the perception, Husserl claims that the "and" is in the
phenomena themselves, and is not something I project onto
them from my own mental acts. Finally (and this is important for
Heidegger) we can reflect even more deeply on the perception
and say that the tree *is* green in the perception. The "is" was also
not obvious in the original perception, yet it was there all along
as well.

Categorial intuition means that every perception consists of layers buried within layers, all of them lying in the perception from
the start, although they are not evident to us without later analysis. This discovery goes a step further than intentionality: not only
are phenomena present to us in consciousness, but more is present
in these phenomena than meets the eye. The phenomena have
greater richness and depth than they seem to have at first.

THE *A PRIORI*

This gives us what Heidegger calls the original sense of the *a priori*. This Latin term is widely used by philosophers, especially Kant,
to describe what comes *before* all experience. In Kant's philosophy,
for example, space and time are *a priori*, because in his view we do
not discover time and space through experience; rather, experience
would not be possible without space and time in the first place.
The usual interpretation of the *a priori* regards it as a term per-
taining to human knowledge. That is to say, many philosophers
think that *a priori* means anything humans *know* before an experience occurs, even if they only know it tacitly in some sort of background manner. According to Heidegger, phenomenology
succeeds in turning this idea upside down. The *a priori* is not what
humans *know* first, but what *is* first. The original sense of the *a priori*, says Heidegger, is a title for being, not for knowing. The *a priori* part of a perception is the deeper layer of categories that a
phenomenon relies on without openly expressing them. For example, in the case of a blue car, blue is *a priori* with respect to the blue
car, and color is *a priori* with respect to the blue and the car, and
"is" is *a priori* with respect to all of them. When I perceive a car I
am probably focused on all its specific details, not on the fact that
it has color or that it simply "is." But if these elements were not
present, my whole perception of the car would be impossible.
Conscious awareness always skates along a thin icy crust, one that

hides countless deeper layers that are also given to us, but not clearly and openly.

BEYOND PHENOMENOLOGY

Heidegger greatly appreciates all three of these insights; the tone of his lecture course is one of admiring celebration, not sour-faced critique. Heidegger does want to push phenomenology to more radical extremes. However, he says quite sincerely that phenomenology already has an inner tendency to go even deeper. Based on the three insights just summarized, Heidegger defines phenomenology as "the analytic description of intentionality in its *a priori*."

Like most of Heidegger's technical phrases, this one is far easier to understand than it sounds. The subject matter of phenomenology is intentionality: the presence of phenomena in consciousness. Our task as phenomenologists is to describe carefully all that is hidden in any act of consciousness, which means that we merely analyze something that we already have. And what we discover by analyzing it are the hidden *a priori* layers that were already there from the start. To repeat, this means that phenomenology is "the analytic description of intentionality in its *a priori*," a phrase that I hope will now be clear. In layman's terms, it simply means that we take any conscious experience and analyze all the hidden layers that it presupposes. This is why Heidegger thinks that the question of the meaning of being arises naturally from Husserl's phenomenology. For what is the one thing presupposed by all conscious experience? *Being*. This green truck *is*. This plate of rigatoni *is*. This boy and this girl *are* cousins. Unfortunately, phenomenology pulls up short before asking more deeply about the meaning of being. We will now see why.

THE QUESTION OF BEING

One of the most important methods of phenomenology is described by the Greek word *epokhe*, which means to abstain or withhold from doing something. If I am a phenomenologist watching all the cars and trucks speeding past my apartment building, the first thing I must do is suspend all belief (or disbelief) in whether those cars and trucks really exist, or whether they might somehow be dreams or illusions. Put differently, a phenomenologist is supposed to *bracket* the existence of the world, or even better, "place it in parentheses." Without doing this, we would remain stuck in various scientific theories about cars, trucks, colors, sounds, and motion. Only by bracketing our perceptions do we stay rigorously focused on the difference between how things appear to us and what we tacitly assume about them. What *appear* to us are the phenomena of cars and trucks: colored silhouettes speeding past us, visible from only one angle at any given moment. What we *assume* is that the cars and trucks really exist, that they are independent three-dimensional objects, and that their invisible backsides are actually there even though we cannot see them right now. This method of bracketing the world is also called *reduction* by phenomenologists: the transcendental reduction, in this case. Reduction turns the entire world, with all its supposed hidden forces and laws, into nothing but a field of phenomena for consciousness.

Phenomenology comes very close to raising the question of being, but not close enough. The discovery of categorial intuition showed that there are always deeper layers within any act of consciousness, layers that are not quite "hidden," but not fully explicit either. Being should be the deepest and most *a priori* layer of all, since everything depends on it. But Husserl never asks about being, and the reason for this turns out to be simple. Husserl is not really concerned with asking about the being of things; he is only concerned with how things can be made the object of a possible rigorous philosophy. The way he achieves this goal is by suspending the reality of all objects and converting them into sheer visible phenomena. The whole point of abstaining and bracketing is to eliminate the independent reality of things, not to preserve it. In a sense, Heidegger sees this as a good thing—after all, Heidegger does not want to define the being of things in scientific terms either, for the same reasons that Husserl did not. But this negative strategy also makes it impossible for Husserl to find any *positive* way to define the being of things. They will always be appearances for human consciousness before they are anything else. By reducing everything to its appearance, phenomenology claimed to be returning "to the things themselves" (Husserl's favorite motto). But in Heidegger's view, reducing things to phenomena does such obvious injustice to the things that Husserl cannot have invented this error on his own. Instead, he must be the unwitting slave of traditional philosophical assumptions. Without realizing it, Husserl is trapped in a philosophical horizon defined more than two thousand years earlier by the ancient Greeks, when the question of being was never raised again after Plato and Aristotle, and was even dismissed as trivial and useless.

To reduce things to phenomena, to bracket the world, is wrong in yet another sense. It suppresses the fact that they are *my* experiences. By reducing my life to a series of appearances of green and brown shapes drifting before my eyes, it merely turns them into a "what," or a set of objective qualities. It turns the whole world into nothing but a series of *essences*, and in this way stifles the *existence* of the things. Phenomenology makes it sound as though I were a calm, antiseptic observer dressed in a white coat, standing on a lofty tower and describing everything neutrally. But there is no such separation between me and the world. It is not I the pure consciousness who encounters the world, but rather I the young professor, or I the haggard drug addict, wounded soldier, expectant mother, cancer patient, or condemned prisoner. By putting essence before existence, quality before being, phenomenology misses the question of being altogether.

We find traces of this criticism in the later existentialism of Jean-Paul Sartre (Heidegger's great admirer) when he announces "existence before essence" as the slogan of his school. Heidegger claims that reducing things to qualities might work if those things were rocks and trees. But what if there were some entity that had no "what," and whose entire reality consisted solely in its act of being? In medieval philosophy, this was said to be God. For Heidegger (as for Sartre) it is human beings who take over this role. Human Dasein can never be reduced to a Spock-like emotionless observer who witnesses colors and shapes, because the very reality of Dasein lies in its inescapable *existence*, deeper than all its specific properties. We are stuck in the world, and we care about it. We are implicated in it.

In one sense, Heidegger claims that Husserl has a hidden tendency to raise the question of being through the theme of categorial intuition. But in another sense, he now states that by reducing the things to phenomena, Husserl is responsible for *losing* the question of being. Phenomenology does give an answer to the question of the meaning of being, but the answer is a bad one: for Husserl, being means nothing but appearance to consciousness. In Heidegger's view, this answer is just as unphilosophical as when the natural sciences reduce objects to their physical qualities. Both science and phenomenology only see things from the outside, failing to grasp their turbulent, ambiguous depths. According to Heidegger, this error is not a personal quirk of Edmund Husserl, nor even a mistake of the entire tradition of Western philosophy. Rather, it is an automatic result of the *fallenness* of Dasein. In an earlier lecture course, we saw that Heidegger spoke of the "ruinance" of Dasein, which is always absorbed in the things of its world and unaware of its own deeper being. In 1926, ruinance has become fallenness, a far more famous Heideggerian term.

1927: Temporality and Being

Heidegger's summer semester course in 1927 was entitled *The Basic Problems of Phenomenology*. Since this was his first full semester following the publication of *Being and Time*, the course coincides with his rapid emergence onto the world philosophical stage. *Basic Problems* shows the same balanced self-confidence and intellectual maturity found in the other works of this period. It is perhaps his best sustained piece of historical analysis, and certainly one of his boldest. Whereas the 1925 course had merely criticized Husserl for reducing reality to its presence in consciousness, the 1927 course widens the attack—the entire history of philosophy is now targeted for having reduced being to presence. Heidegger focuses on four illuminating historical examples of this process.

WAYS OF OVERLOOKING BEING

First, there is Kant's claim that "being is not a real predicate": in other words, Kant holds that one hundred real dollars contain nothing more than one hundred imaginary dollars. The difference between them, for Kant, lies only in the fact that in the two cases, the hundred dollars have a different "position" with respect to us: in one case they are linked to other objects in the world, and in the other they exist solely in our minds. Second, Heidegger criticizes the famous medieval distinction between the existence and the essence of a thing. Third, he attacks the split made by Descartes between two kinds of being: physical extension and human thought. Finally, he criticizes the idea of being as a "copula" found in Thomas Hobbes and other philosophers. The copula in grammar is simply the connection between a subject and a predicate: if we say "the tree is dead," the word "is" exists only to connect the words "tree" and "dead." According to Hobbes, the word "is" has no special meaning in itself.

Heidegger criticizes all four of these concepts quite brilliantly, and any interested reader is encouraged to read the entire lecture course to see how. But his basic point in all four cases is the same. In each example, being is treated as a simple, obvious, boring kind of presence—either presence for human consciousness, or physical presence within the universe. There is no attempt to consider being in its dark and stormy character as a partly concealed event, act, or performance. None of the theories he criticizes understand that Dasein is deeply enmeshed in its world in a partly mysterious way, and that no set of descriptive features can ever do justice either to Dasein or its world.

Put differently, each of the four criticized positions think of the question of being as a simple yes/no question. Either a thing exists or not: end of story. But for Heidegger, being is never a yes/no question: to be always means to be in a highly specific way, different for each thing that exists. It always entails a partial absence from view rather than a simple lucid presence ("yes") or failure to be present ("no").

THE ONTOLOGICAL DIFFERENCE

Following three hundred pages of devastating historical analysis, Heidegger aims to replace the traditional concepts of presence and production with his own concept of temporality. He does this by using one concept that becomes a durable element of his thinking, and another that turns out to be a short-lived experiment. The more long-lived of the two is known as the "ontological difference," or the difference between being and beings.

To a large extent, the ontological difference follows naturally from Heidegger's reading of categorial intuition. Although the individual things we encounter can be called beings in the plural, all of them already contain being in the singular as their deeper ground. To clear up a possible confusion, it should be noted that Heidegger speaks of being in two different ways. In one sense there is being as the single reality that is asked about in the question of the meaning of being. This question takes no notice of the numerous specific things that exist, and merely asks for the meaning of being, plain and simple. But at the same time, Heidegger also speaks of the being of *specific* entities. The secret of a great biologist, mathematician, or historian is that they redefine the being of the specific beings they work with, without ever asking the question of being in general.

For example, the astronomer Johannes Kepler redefined planetary orbits from circles into ellipses in which the sun lies at one focus. To do this, he had to rethink the *being* of planetary orbits, disclosing their inner nature in a new way. But this does not mean that Kepler posed the question of being in general, as a revolutionary philosopher would. We humans are able to rethink the being of beings only because we are not merely trapped on the level of things as they appear to us. Instead, we have already partly risen above the appearances that surround us, and already peer to some extent into their depths. Otherwise, it would be impossible to gain any knowledge about anything at all, and we would be stupefied in every moment by the immediate data of our senses. As Heidegger puts it, this means that Dasein displays the feature of *transcendence*. Transcendence does not just happen every once in awhile in lucky moments, but must happen at all moments in order for human experience to occur in the first place.

For Heidegger, to exist means to perform the ontological difference. Animals cannot do this, and hence animals cannot liberate the previously concealed being of any kind of being and make it the object of knowledge. But this is exactly what human scientists do. Science manages to objectify some layer of reality that was somehow already vaguely revealed beforehand; if it had not already been revealed in some vague, preliminary way, science would never have been able to discover it. Science slowly objectifies the things that human Dasein is already loosely aware of, and makes it the object of an organized theory.

Heidegger's own example from the history of science is Galileo. Before Galileo, humans were obviously aware that objects in nature could be measured mathematically. Scientists had been measuring the speeds and sizes of objects for quite some time. However, it was Galileo who first pursued the project of mathematizing the whole of nature in a systematic way, so that all the pre-Galilean scientific concepts were replaced by a mathematical measurement of nature. An additional step was taken by Descartes, when he defined the being of physical nature as nothing but matter taking up space and pushing against other matter as it enters new spaces. When this happened, the former Aristotelian concepts of physics were set aside, and nature was redefined as nothing but matter occupying spatial positions and measurable in mathematical terms. This was possible because of the way that the being of nature was disclosed and objectified by modern science.

Just as science objectifies beings, philosophy tries to objectify being itself. From amidst the swirling ambiguity and confusion of our world, Plato objectified the world as perfect forms inhabiting corrupt physical matter, and Leibniz objectified it as made up of indivisible "monads" unable to relate to each other and linked only through the power of God. The basic act of any philosophy, any ontology, is to project the essence of being in terms of some concept.

As might be imagined, objectification has its good side and its bad side. In an obvious sense, it is apparently better to be Galileo, Descartes, or Plato and objectify the world according to some new concept than to be a lazy, opinionated slacker who takes everything as it comes without taking any theoretical risk. The objectification of the world can be a heroic achievement; all of the great moments in intellectual history are objectifications, as is all human thought more generally. But the bad side is also easy to see. To objectify something means to oversimplify it, turning it into a caricature. When Newton defined the world as made up of universal attraction between masses, he objectified physical bodies and asked us to exclude all the specific details of these bodies so that they would fit his theory. This had brilliant and useful results in Newton's case. Yet it can also become a dogma that suppresses all aspects of the world that escape the theory, thereby creating obstacles to potential works of genius in the future. It took someone of the stature of Einstein to oppose Newton's assumption that gravity works instantly, and to show the implications that follow if gravity can only work at the speed of light. The same could be said of Darwin's concept of evolution by natural selection: Darwin's theory is a stunning intellectual monument that continues to suggest new ideas even today. Yet to some extent it also closes our eyes to other mechanisms that may be at work in nature (such as the formation of new species of life through symbiosis) and which may cut against the grain of the survival of the fittest as the mechanism for evolution. Any monumental scientific discovery will always tend to become a dogma that cruelly suppresses counterexamples in order to consolidate its vision of the world.

In Heidegger's view, the danger of objectification for philosophy is even simpler, and even more dangerous. When being is objectified, what always happens is that some specific being is identified with being itself. This began at the dawn of philosophy, when Thales of Miletus (sixth century BC) said that the first principle of everything is water. For Thales, water is not just one type of thing within the world, but rather the uniquely special and privileged thing that explains all the rest. A bit later, Democritus said the same thing about atoms. Heidegger and his postmodern admirers call this process "ontotheology," since most philosophies claim to be a neutral study of being, but raise some *particular* being (such as water) to the godlike status of explaining all the rest. Heidegger sees the history of philosophy as riddled with ontotheology from one end to the other. In his view, ontology should never raise one particular being to the status of being itself. The only way to avoid this mistake is to insist on the ontological difference: the constant shadowy interplay between concealed being and any particular beings that emerge. According to Heidegger, this interplay should now become the central topic of philosophy.

In other words, philosophy must be recentered in the concept of *time*. We already know that Heidegger does not view time as a series of "nows" counted by a watch or even by an atomic clock. Time simply refers to the mysterious way in which everything that appears or comes to presence is shadowed by a bottomless depth of concealed reality—every moment is an event, and an event is never fully visible, definable, or describable. The only way to get at the depths of the world is through interpretation, not direct vision. Categorial intuition showed us that there are always concealed layers in any perception, and Heidegger says that time is the ultimate concealed layer of everything. As he puts it, time is the primary or transcendental horizon of ontology.

TEMPORALITY WITH A CAPITAL "T"

We now come to the second new concept in this lecture course, the one that did not survive into later writings. When Heidegger speaks of the temporality of Dasein, his usual word for temporality is the normal German term *Zeitlichkeit*. In this lecture course, he once again takes a stab at using Latinate terminology to point to a deeper level of his analysis (which is somewhat surprising, given his usual contempt for Latin as intellectually inferior to Greek). The words Heidegger uses here are *Temporalität, Praesens,* and *Absens,* easily recognizable to speakers of English as "temporality," "presence," and "absence." *Temporalität* is usually capitalized in English as "Temporality" to distinguish it from the other word for temporality.

Heidegger describes Temporality with a capital "T" as the most original temporalization of temporality. Another name for it is "ecstatic" time, referring to a kind of time that does not stand motionless in some central moment, but constantly stands outside itself. Heidegger gives here a new analysis of equipment, which should mostly be left until the chapter on *Being and Time* where it belongs. He focuses on the experience of finding something missing from a system of tools: some objects are ready-to-hand, while others are unavailable. Things are already there for us in our environment, but are also interpreted by us "as" being such and such. The combination of these two moments gives us the present. This threefold structure is ecstatic temporality, in which the single appearance of a thing is already torn in two separate directions. We have heard similar ideas several times already in Heidegger's career, and so this one comes as no great surprise. But Heidegger now tries to go a step further by saying that ecstatic temporality has a deeper horizon, and that this horizon can be defined as either *Praesens* or *Absens,* depending on whether we are speaking of the presence or absence of the thing from the environment. Whether this is a useful step or not (and my bet is "not useful," since he never tried it again) what is most interesting is to notice Heidegger's strategy. What he is trying to do is to move into ever-deeper layers of Dasein's being by proceeding through a series of stages or "horizons."

First, there is our understanding of beings in the world, since everyone has a loose familiarity with clouds, trees, and the sun. Second, there is the act of projecting the being of things according to some specific concept of them, which we see very clearly in the case of scientists such as Kepler and Newton when they redefine various things in our environment. Third, Dasein must already have some half-clear understanding of being, for without this understanding we could never make projections of the being of specific entities. Finally, he says that there is projection upon time, since we cannot understand being as a single static lump, but only in an ambiguous, threefold sense. At this stage, Heidegger says, we have almost reached the philosophical bedrock of the universe. The only way to go any deeper would be to discuss the finitude of time itself—showing that time is not the ultimate layer of the universe, but that it rests on an even further, deeper horizon. For the second time, we have here a foretaste of Heidegger's concept of *nothingness*, to be described in detail below. If time is only a finite part of reality, this is because it exists against a deeper background of nothingness.

Temporality is always richer than any particular thing that arises from it. Being is always richer than beings. The possible is always richer than the actual. Beings are always richer than any objectification of them. All of these consequences stem from Heidegger's radicalizing of the philosophy of Husserl, for whom categorial intuition is always deeper than the presence of phenomena in consciousness.

1928: Human Transcendence

The lecture course known in English as *Metaphysical Foundations of Logic* (often nicknamed "The Leibniz Course") was the final course Heidegger gave in Marburg: the last fruit of this key period of his career, and one of the ripest. The first part of the course discusses the great German philosopher G. W. Leibniz (1646–1716). In the early twentieth century there had been attempts to show that Leibniz was mostly a logician, and that his metaphysics or general theory of reality was grounded in his ideas about logic. Heidegger wants to reverse this priority and show that logic is always grounded in metaphysics or ontology, not the other way around. Logic turns out to be possible only on the basis of a deeper human transcendence of the world. This transcendence is the topic of the second half of the lecture course, which will be our focus here.

FUNDAMENTAL ONTOLOGY

Heidegger describes his own method of philosophy, at this stage, as fundamental ontology. And fundamental ontology, he says, is obliged to interpret Dasein in terms of temporality; otherwise, we are back in Husserl's model of the presence of things in consciousness, if not something even worse. But if Dasein is temporal, this implies that Dasein's understanding of being has a historical character: philosophy is never a set of final true results, but always a brave and unpredictable foray into the concealed depths of the world, which is a triple-faced event rather than something simply present. This leads Heidegger to attack the usual way of presenting philosophy in textbooks. Philosophy teachers tend to slice philosophy into a set of well-known "problems," which in Heidegger's opinion simply drains the life out of philosophy. In fact, new beginnings for philosophy are always possible in the future, and will always be completely unforeseeable, because they rise from deep caverns into which no one can ever fully descend.

For similar reasons, any great philosophy will always be much deeper than its contemporary readers realize. When a new philosophy appears, we are likely to reduce it to a list of viewpoints and opinions that it contains, yet the hidden depth of the philosophy will always exceed any such list. To use Heidegger's own example, even the great Kant was refuted left and right by those in his own time, yet most of these critics are forgotten and irrelevant today, while the Kantian earthquake continues to shake the world more than two hundred years later. A philosopher is really only understood by the generations that come later.

TRANSCENDENCE

The question of being can only be understood through Dasein's transcendence. Dasein does not just observe phenomena and remain duped by their shimmering surfaces. Instead, Dasein always rises above beings and has some understanding of their being. In fact, Dasein even transcends itself: we do not just take our own inner lives at face value, but also engage in complicated introspection, undergo psychotherapy, or even (if we have sufficient talent) invent entirely new schools of psychology from scratch. Dasein is actually *nothing but* transcendence. Here Heidegger remarks, with obvious annoyance, that Husserl had rejected the concept of transcendence when it was proposed to him two years earlier. As he sees it, this is Husserl's loss, and Husserl will have to suffer the consequences of missing this key feature of human being. Dasein is not an "intraworldly being" like trees and hammers: these entities merely sit inside the world, without *being in the world* like human Dasein, which is openly aware of the world and struggles with it. There is something quite special about Dasein, and this can only be found in its transcendence. Only Dasein rises above the world, unlike tools, physical objects, or even animals. Dasein is inherently something alien to nature; human existence is a fateful tear or rupture in the fabric of the world.

FREEDOM

Another name for transcendence is *freedom*. Dasein is nothing but its freedom, because only Dasein rises above the things of the world and grasps them in their being. As Heidegger will say at the end of the course, Dasein is a creature of distance, able to back away from the world to some extent. And only through distance do we gain a true nearness to things, as opposed to the false nearness that treats things as nothing but their presence in consciousness, or the false nearness of radios, telephones, and other technological devices. Here, we find that Heidegger's later obsession with the crisis of global technology has already begun to emerge.

Although temporality consists of three moments, all of them apparently equal, Heidegger often claims that the future has a certain priority. The reason for this should be clear, now that we have considered the transcendence and freedom of Dasein. The engine that drives the threefold structure of time is the fact that Dasein always partly rises above what is present, and thereby sets the threefold interplay of temporality into motion. Dasein transcends because it recognizes the finitude of beings, by grasping the deeper horizon lying beyond them.

Ultimately, this means that Dasein is a creature of nothingness. Dasein "nihilates" beings by rising above them and seeing that they are not all that they claimed to be, or perhaps that they are more than they claimed to be—by grasping them in their deeper being instead of just taking them at face value. Only because Dasein transcends and nihilates can Dasein ever ask "why?" about anything. The question "why?" obviously requires transcendence, since when we ask "why?" we are passing beyond whatever is immediately given and looking for a deeper, underlying ground. The fact that being must also appear, not just hide, is unavoidable. Everything real is accompanied by appearance or semblance, and this often makes it difficult to separate philosophy from sophistry. Dasein is a creature of freedom and depth, a creature that surpasses the world toward its possibilities, but at the same time Dasein is also a creature of semblance and false nearness. Animals are not philosophers, but neither are they sophists; humans can sink beneath the lowest animals just as often as they rise to the greatest heights.

METONTOLOGY

We now come to Heidegger's famous handful of pages on "metontology." While this concept is not placed at the very end of the course, it is perhaps the most intriguing concept in the lectures, and is therefore a good note on which to end our summary of the 1928 course. The word *metontology* refers to the Greek word *metabole*, an important concept in Aristotle's *Physics* that is still recognizable in the English word "metabolism." *Metabole* means change or turnabout. For Heidegger, metontology is not something higher or deeper than normal ontology, but is in some ways even "lower." Metontology is the collapse of ontology back into the specific regions of life that it initially tried to surpass. Whereas ontology deals in broad and seemingly abstract terms with the entire world, metontology (Heidegger merely proposes it, and never develops it) is supposed to deal with more concrete topics. Although Heidegger only gives two examples of such topics, they are literally infinite in number. Only metontology would allow us to pass from Heidegger's high-flying ontological concepts back down to possible philosophical theories of art, animal life, political reality, human psychology, military strategy, or any specific topic one might imagine. As it turns out, the two he actually mentions are *ethics* and *sexual difference*. Only metontology could give us a rigorous philosophical treatment of ethics, and only metontology could shed philosophical light on the difference between the sexes, which is (by necessity) completely missing from Heidegger's own analyses of Dasein.

THE TURN

Heidegger says that metontology will not only cause a reversal of ontology into the concrete realm, but will also lead to a *turn* in ontology. He does not specify what this means, but the German word he uses for "turn" is *Kehre*. This is interesting, since *Kehre* is the same word Heidegger sometimes uses to describe the later turn in his own philosophical thinking (which is dated at different times by different scholars).

METAPHYSICS

Heidegger says that by combining ontology with metontology, we get the whole of *metaphysics*. Metaphysics belongs to the very essence of human Dasein. The reader should be aware that this is one of the last times that Heidegger ever uses the word "metaphysics" in a positive sense as a name for philosophical speculation. In later years, he increasingly uses "metaphysics" as a term of contempt for those philosophies that remain trapped in ontotheology: philosophies that define being itself in terms of one specific kind of being: whether it be water, air, atoms, thinking substance, absolute spirit, will to power, or intentionality.

The end of this lecture course also marked the end of Heidegger's career in Marburg. Still a young man, he was called to the last and highest academic position of his career, as Husserl's successor in Freiburg. In many ways this was a dream come true. Just ten years earlier (in 1918), Heidegger was merely a talented but obscure assistant who idolized Husserl but had not yet won the master's full respect. Only a decade later, Heidegger returned to Freiburg in glory: not only as the new occupant of Husserl's important chair, but also as the most celebrated philosopher in Europe. The next twenty years would not be so lucky.

4

Being and Time

Being and Time is the greatest book of philosophy written in the twentieth century, and probably the greatest work of systematic philosophy since Hegel's *Phenomenology of Spirit* in 1807. Originally, the title page of the book said "Being and Time: First Half," and was still printed this way for many years. Eventually, Heidegger dropped the claim that a second half would ever appear, since after so much time had passed it would be impossible to publish a second half without reworking the first. Many scholars have noted that all the topics Heidegger promised for the second half were covered in other writings. In this sense, *Being and Time* is not actually an unfinished book. Even so, the public expectation that a second half would appear must have caused Heidegger some stress over the next quarter century until he finally dropped the claim.

The book begins with perhaps the most famous dedication page in the history of philosophy: "To Edmund Husserl, in Friendship and Admiration." But we also need to imagine the book with a second, suppressed dedication written in invisible ink: a dedication to his former mistress Hannah Arendt, whom Heidegger privately described as the inspiration of the book. In this sense *Being and Time* presents a small paradox. In the recent history of philosophy, perhaps only Nietzsche's books have a deeper tone of loneliness than *Being and Time*, in which Dasein stands ever alone before anxiety, nothingness, and death. Nonetheless, the book was written in close proximity to two of the major intellectual figures of the twentieth century. Few of the greatest works of philosophy have enjoyed the luxury of such close intellectual companionship of such a high caliber, however negative Husserl's view of the book may have been.

The greatness of this work lies in its depth and simplicity. Heidegger states that the question of being has been forgotten since the days of ancient Greece. Being is now assumed to be something present for human view, or physically present: being is spirit, or atoms, or God, or will to power, or phenomena in consciousness. For this reason, many people even think that the question of being is the most useless and empty of all questions. But for Heidegger it is the most important question of all. In *Being and Time*, Heidegger wants to revive the forgotten question of being through an analysis of human existence. He chooses Dasein as his topic because only Dasein can ask the question of being in the first place; to understand what the question of being means, we first have to understand the structure of Dasein.

An even more important virtue of Dasein is that human being is more difficult to interpret in terms of presence than any other entity. True enough, we can always view humans from the outside, describing their appearance, their mannerisms, their personality types, and their exact height, weight, and DNA profile. But this will only be something external, since it tells us nothing about what it is actually like to *live* the life of any particular Dasein. No Dasein is a mere set of visible properties: Dasein can only be understood as the event, act, or performance of its own being. It is never entirely visible from the outside. We are not even entirely visible to our own selves, since we all struggle with the obscure complexities of introspection.

Heidegger says that the "horizon" of the question of the meaning of being is none other than *time*. When he says that time is the horizon, this means that only within the concept of time can we reach any proper understanding of being at all. The reader is reminded that Heidegger is not referring to chronological time on the clock or calendar, but rather "kairological" time, an ambiguous threefold structure found in any moment whatsoever. But Heidegger means something even deeper than this. It is not just that Dasein only *understands* being through the concept of time. We find a stronger and more compelling interpretation by Hans-Georg Gadamer (1900–2002) in his major work *Truth and Method*. Gadamer observes that for Heidegger, the point is not only that time is the *horizon* of being: for Heidegger, being itself *is* time. This means that being itself is never simply present, but is always an ambiguous threefold structure. This threefold belongs to being itself, not just to human understanding.

The Question of Being

"For apparently you have long been aware of what you mean when you use the word *being*. We, however, who used to think we understood it, have become confused." This quotation from Plato's dialogue *Sophist* is selected by Heidegger for the opening words of his own great book. It is hard to imagine a better choice. In posing the question of the meaning of being, Heidegger realizes that many people consider it not to be a real question at all. The first task of his book is to reawaken the *need* for this question, which has withered away since the high period of ancient Greek philosophy.

The objections to the question of being take three closely linked forms: being is the most universal concept, being is indefinable, and being is self-evident. In other words, since all of our talk about anything at all presupposes the concept of being, there is no way to define it. Therefore, to ask about being is a waste of time. The reader may have guessed that all three of these objections will be exposed as attempts to view being as *presence*. Presence is the enemy we must slay before there is any hope of reviving ontology.

Dasein Must Be Interrogated

There follows Heidegger's famous but somewhat tedious claim that every question has three parts: that which is asked about, that which is interrogated, and that which is to be found out by the asking. (The elegance of the original German trio cannot be reproduced in English: *das Gefragte, das Befragte, das Erfragte.*) Few passages in Heidegger strike beginners as more dazzlingly subtle than this one. But on closer examination, we simply have our old friend the threefold temporal structure. Every question analyzes something that is already given to us (past: the interrogated), in order to find out something new (future: that which is to be found out), with the resulting combination giving us the question as a whole (present: that which is asked about). Far more interesting is Heidegger's decision about which entity should be "interrogated" in the question of being. He begins by saying that *beings* must be interrogated to learn about their being. But just one paragraph later, it is human Dasein alone that is hauled in for questioning. Since it is humans who ask the question of the meaning of being, he thinks that we need to clarify the being of the human questioner in order to understand the question properly. Even so, this can only be a first step. As Heidegger memorably puts it: the being of beings is not itself a being.

We now seem to be trapped in a circle. To pose the question of being, we begin by trying to clarify the being of Dasein. Yet how can we do this if we do not already know what being is in the first place? This is similar to the paradox that arises in Plato's great dialogue *Meno.* The Sophists think it is a waste of time to look for virtue: after all, if we already know what virtue is there is no point in looking for it, and if we do not know then we will not be able to recognize it when we find it. Heidegger's response is essentially the same as that of Socrates to the Sophists: we do know what being (or virtue) is in advance, but only in a vague, partially defined way, and not yet as the rigorous concept that we seek. In present-day philosophy this is often called the "hermeneutic circle," or circle of interpretation. It is obviously an important concept for Heidegger, as seen in his views on how science and all forms of knowledge work. We must always have a hazy, prescientific grasp of the being of plants, animals, or comets for the scientist to be able to project this being in a new and more lucid way.

To repeat, the analysis of human Dasein is only meant to pave the way for a discussion of being itself. This is why Heidegger rejected the charge of Husserl and others that he had slipped away from philosophy toward a kind of anthropology of Dasein. Human being only serves as an avenue toward being.

ONTOLOGICAL AND ONTIC

Heidegger makes an important distinction between the terms *ontological* and *ontic.* "Ontological," of course, refers to anything that deals with being. "Ontic," by contrast, pertains to specific beings. He gives a quick example of the distinction by observing that while Dasein is *ontically* closer to us than any other being (since we ourselves are Dasein), it is ontologically the furthest from us. On the one hand, I have an abundance of information about myself and the other Daseins that are known to me. On the other hand, all of this information is a purely external list of features and traits that have nothing to do with the being of Dasein. For the most part, we find ourselves absorbed with *other* entities in the world, and pay little heed to the actual structure of Dasein's existence.

THE TEMPORALITY OF DASEIN

The initial aim of the book is to show that temporality is the meaning of the being of Dasein. It will turn out, now as ever, that Dasein is not something clearly and lucidly present. Instead, Dasein is deployed in a threefold form of ecstatic time that stands outside of itself by simultaneously swinging toward the past and future. Since Dasein is the one who asks the question of being, it follows that time will be the horizon for the understanding of being as a whole.

DESTRUCTION OF THE HISTORY OF ONTOLOGY

The introduction to *Being and Time* raises another important theme: the need for a destruction of the history of ontology. The word deconstruction would probably work just as well, but Heidegger says *Destruktion* in German, and it is also best not to assume total agreement between Heidegger and his French deconstructionist admirers (Jacques Derrida above all). Dasein does not see the world directly, because Dasein has a historical structure, and generally interprets things in the same way that others interpret them. In the West, our usual clichéd or received interpretation of the world is dominated by the Greek tradition of philosophy. And even for the Greeks, but especially for their European heirs, being is always some kind of presence. This presence takes on numerous different forms at various times in the history of philosophy. The history of ontology needs to be painstakingly destroyed, as strange as that may sound. When we destroy it we do not smash it to rubble and cease to study it, but simply expose its inner structural skeleton.

This does not sound like a modest project, and it is not meant to be. Despite a few awkward gestures of humility in the introduction, Heidegger is quite sure that his book marks a turning point in the entire history of philosophy. But at least he is willing to admit that he stands in a specific historic time and place; for this reason he realizes that he is limited, unable to jump over his own shadow. Unlike countless other great philosophers, Heidegger does not believe that his own philosophy is the final one.

Tools and Broken Tools

Dasein is not a sterilized thinking machine who gazes calmly at the world. Dasein is in each case *mine*; "mineness" is in fact its key feature. What distinguishes Dasein from bicycles, mushrooms, or even dogs is that Dasein's own being is always an issue for it. I am constantly occupied with my own being, and with how things are going for that being. Dasein is not made up of a list of qualities: its essence is nothing but existence. Only Dasein has existence, and only Dasein has mineness. We can also say that Dasein has a special relationship to its possibilities. Whereas flowers or clods of dirt have possibilities that we might include in a list of visible qualities, Dasein *is* its possibilities, since it is constantly occupied with them. Furthermore, Dasein can exist either authentically or inauthentically: I can either truly come to grips with my own deepest possibility of being, or draw my ambitions and self-understanding from what the public says.

Average Everydayness

Heidegger insists that the proper way to gain a philosophical understanding of Dasein is not to look for a special case of it. We should neither analyze unique examples of heroic scientific and political Dasein, nor look for some "primitive" Dasein amidst the tribes of a rain forest. Instead, we should consider Dasein in its "average everydayness." Only by looking at the undistinguished case of normal, everyday Dasein can we gain insight into the features that belong to every Dasein. But we must never forget that Dasein is a "who," which means an event, action, or performance, and not a "what" that can be seen from the outside. This sweeping caveat rules out every past interpretation of human being, especially the two most influential: the Greek concept of humans as rational animals, and the Christian idea of humans as created in the image of God. Both of these notions reduce Dasein to an entity that has certain properties that are viewed from the outside. In this way, they fail to do justice to Dasein in its innermost being.

BEING-IN-THE-WORLD

Human beings are not just ghosts floating through the world and gazing upon objects. Dasein is always being-in-the-world, and inseparable from the world. Even though Dasein and world must be different in some sense, being-in-the-world is a unified structure. It is important here to specify what the word "in" means. Usually "in" refers to something spatially present inside of another thing. Water is in a glass, New Orleans is in the state of Louisiana, a soul is somehow in a body. This is not what being-in-the-world means. Instead, being-in means that Dasein is immersed in the world, involved with it, permanently intertwined and occupied with it even when it feels alienated or lonely. For this very reason, Heidegger says that only Dasein can touch other entities, since only Dasein has access to them or is truly aware of them. A chair can never touch a wall, because these objects have no way of encountering one another, even if their physical bodies are in direct contact.

As we learned from Heidegger in his earlier years, Dasein is always marked by *facticity*. It does not exist as an independent thing hovering in a void, but always finds itself in a particular situation with highly specific possibilities. For the most part, this facticity does not take the form of *knowledge*. Too many philosophers have constructed their model of human being by imagining humans as entities that *know* the world. Heidegger sees that knowing is only a rare special case of the way that we deal with our environment, as his tool-analysis will brilliantly show. Knowledge is not primary, because it arises from out of the world. Dasein somehow has to rise above its usual interaction with the world in order to gain anything resembling knowledge. Dasein and world are bound together closely from the start. If this seems to eliminate the traditional problem in philosophy of how human beings can know a world lying outside of them, then so much the better. For Heidegger as for Husserl, this is a false problem that never should have existed in the first place.

To describe the two parts of being-in-the-world, it is easier to begin with the world—which means the entities within the world. Not surprisingly, Heidegger says that entities should not be described as physically present-at-hand or as phenomena viewed by consciousness. We need to look at how Dasein actually encounters entities "for the most part," in its average everyday-ness. The "worldhood" of the world, as Heidegger terms it, is a structure that belongs only to Dasein, not to other entities in iso-lation from humans. This is the reason that *Being and Time* ana-lyzes Dasein rather than trees, factories, or atoms. The usual idea of the world as "nature" must be rejected (just as Husserl would reject it) because the concept of nature arises from our average way of encountering entities. We need to look at the environ-ment and how Dasein deals with it. Things are not present-at-hand in this environment, but are usually encountered as *equipment.*

THE READY-TO-HAND

For the most part, Dasein encounters entities that are not present-at-hand, but ready-to-hand. Dasein does not usually stare at things or analyze them theoretically, but uses them and takes them for granted. In any given moment, most of us are not thinking about the chair we are sitting in, the floor that supports it, the solid earth beneath the floor, the oxygen we breathe, or the heart and kidneys that keep us alive. Instead, we take these things for granted and focus our attention elsewhere. There is no such thing as "an" equipment, since all equipment is assigned to other equipment in a single gigantic system of references. A house refers to bad weather and to Dasein's need to stay dry; the need to stay dry refers to our medical knowledge; this knowledge refers in turn to our fear of illness and to the ambitions that might be derailed by early death. The number of mutual references of equipment is infi-nite, and all equipment makes up a unified whole. In order to be what they are, tools must recede from visibility. The outward appearance of a thing does not give us an understanding of ready-to-hand entities—tools are not meant for looking at, since we usu-ally just silently rely on them.

Furthermore, the significance of entities is not invented by Dasein in monkish solitude: equipment always belongs to a public world. For some people, sunset refers simply to peace and calm and the end of a long hard day, while for other Daseins it signifies the end of fasting during Ramadan. The readiness-to-hand of equip-ment is what we encounter first; it is not something that we inject into things after first seeing them as bare physical lumps. In fact, what we encounter initially is the world as a whole, not a group of scattered individual things that need to be woven together. Not only is Dasein woven together with the world—all parts of the world are fused into a colossal web of meaning in which everything refers to everything else.

BROKEN TOOLS

Of course, it is not quite this simple. Yes, equipment usually hides from us. It is inconspicuous or unobtrusive. Usually, only bad equipment makes us notice it frequently, such as when ceilings are too low and we bump our heads too often. But equipment also malfunctions sometimes. Cars break down; hammers fall apart or wine glasses shatter; bodily organs suddenly fail us. It is mostly in these moments that equipment first becomes conspicuous and draws our attention to it. There is also the case of tools that turn up missing: when our car is stolen, the bus fails to arrive, or we find that we have misplaced our shoes before leaving for work, these items of equipment are no longer quietly serviceable, but loudly announce their reality.

All such cases make tools present. However, it does not make them purely present-at-hand, since they are still deeply intertwined with world and significance: the broken hammer or vandalized windshield are now annoying pieces of failed equipment that we would like to shove aside. But normally, the items in the world *do not* announce themselves in this way. This is not merely a negative feature, but a positive one, since tools are actually getting something done while they fail to announce themselves. This brilliant tool-analysis is perhaps the greatest moment of twentieth-century philosophy. Its primary target is obviously Husserl. What comes first are not phenomena that appear to consciousness. Phenomena are only rare cases of visible things emerging from a dominant silent background of equipment.

SIGNS AND SIGNALS

Heidegger speaks of another special case of readiness-to-hand: signs and signals. He refers to the automobiles of his time, which had just begun to use primitive turn signals in the form of adjustable red arrows. These arrows indicate the region of space where Dasein plans to turn its vehicle. Unlike the normal case of equipment, the turn signal does not unconsciously direct us toward the region where it wants us to look. Instead, the signaling arrow remains visible, openly declaring itself as a sign that wants us to notice one specific direction rather than the others. By contrast, a hammer is usually not a sign—unless an archaeologist interprets it as a sign that Neanderthals once camped here.

Most equipment disappears from view, but a sign or signal is equipment viewed "as" equipment. This is true even of tools whose use is unknown to us. If we enter a strange laboratory and fail to understand the purpose of all the vats and cages, or if we open up a television and have no idea what each of the parts do, we still understand that all of these things are equipment. We do not think of them as random lumps of plastic and metal, but either ask an expert to explain them, or turn away in boredom and despair. Just as with equipment, an entity's use as a sign is not something projected onto it after we first encounter it as a mere physical lump. Heidegger asks us to imagine that a peasant regards the south wind as a sign that rain is coming. In this case, the peasant encounters the wind as a sign from the start. He does not just feel a rush of air in his face and later add the judgment that "rain must be coming." Everything happens simultaneously.

FOR-THE-SAKE-OF-WHICH

Each item of equipment has a "towards-which": a purpose that it serves. And just as each item of equipment dominates its smaller parts, so too every tool is dissolved into larger systems of purposes. But this process comes to an end somewhere—if not, nothing would ever be visible. The end point of the total system of equipment, according to Heidegger, is called the "for-the-sake-of-which," which is Dasein itself. In other words, all equipment ultimately gains meaning from its purpose in the life of Dasein, the final term in the series. Every entity we encounter gains its ultimate meaning for us from our own being. If we find water at a desert oasis, we do not just describe the water in terms of visible qualities, but feel a sense of thrill at the opportunity to quench our thirst. If we see a hawk or eagle soaring in the sky, this gives us a sense of poetic majesty only because we are not mice or sparrows, for whom these birds of prey are a mortal threat. Everything that we encounter appears as "for-the-sake-of" Dasein—not because it all exists just to serve our purposes, but because we are human, and entities make sense to us only within a total system of human meaning.

SPACE AND PLACE

We should also speak briefly about the spatiality of equipment. This has nothing to do with its presence-at-hand in a distinct geometric location. The space of equipment is above all a *place*—a place in which it has a specific relation to all other equipment. The spatiality of my house is not defined by how many kilometers it is from the capital. Instead, its space is defined by its "sunny side," "shady side," and other terms that relate to my use of it in my life. We define distances in vague terms such as "a good walk," "a stone's throw," or "as long as it takes to smoke a pipe." Even if we say that something is "an hour away," this is not a chronological measurement, but more a kind of rough estimate that suggests how quick or how boring the trip will feel. Long journeys often seem shorter than ones that are objectively short, since length is primarily defined by Dasein's existence, not by exact measurements. For example, a moment ago I was thinking of my computer screen rather than the glasses on my face, even though the glasses are much closer to me in physical terms. While walking on the sidewalk, the friend I see two blocks away is closer than the pavement on which I stand. We only reach exact measurements of space by depriving place of its worldhood.

The true spatiality of Dasein has two aspects: de-severance and directionality. "De-severance" is perhaps the most horrible English term in MacQuarrie and Robinson's version of *Being and Time*, but many readers gradually acquire a taste for it. It is the translators' clever (if unavoidably ugly) attempt to deal with Heidegger's word *Ent-fernung*. Without the hyphen, this is a normal German word meaning "removal" or "distance." Skipping any detailed discussion of how German grammar works, it is enough to say that Heidegger coined this term (by adding the hyphen) in order to refer simultaneously to intensifying distance *and* eliminating it. This is not as paradoxical as it may sound. When I look at a far-off lighthouse, I am seeing it at a great distance—but at the same time it is also in direct, intimate contact with me, since I am occupied with seeing it. Any object that we encounter is de-severed: it is placed at a specific distance, but also brought directly and immediately into our explicit awareness.

The term "directionality" is much easier to understand, since each thing we encounter obviously comes from a specific region, and does not fill up all portions of our existence at once. Some threats approach us from the west, others from the north. But even if the threat is internal to my mind and comes from no direction on the compass, it still comes from only one specific part of my life rather than others. For example, if we are terrified of making public speeches, this threatens only one particular part of our lives. Fear of making the speech does not also make us afraid of swimming, or make us worry that our house has been burglarized during the lecture trip.

Fallenness and Care

Dasein is absorbed in the world, fascinated by it. Dasein is a self that remains the same over time, even though it is not a substantial piece of matter. Yet we are not alone: there are the other Daseins who exist with us. Heidegger rightly notes that I do not usually distinguish myself from the others—rather, the others are mostly those from whom I *do not* distinguish myself. I am one of them, not different from them. The others are co-Dasein, and like me they are also encountered in a specific environment, not in isolation. Just as with equipment, I do not encounter other Daseins as pieces of physical flesh and blood, but meet them in the midst of their labors, wrapped up in the evironment. Even if I meet other Daseins who are doing nothing at all, they are still not encountered as present-at-hand. Rather (in one of the few amusing remarks in his otherwise somber book) Heidegger says that idle Daseins are encountered in an "uncircumspective tarrying alongside everything and nothing."

If "concern" is what we feel for pieces of equipment, what we feel for other Daseins is called "solicitude." Solicitude can be either harmful or helpful. The harmful kind leaps in and relieves the other Dasein of its responsibility, and thereby secretly dominates the other. But the other kind of solicitude leaps ahead and restores the other Dasein's care to it in authentic form for the first time. Although Heidegger does not elaborate with any specific examples, this remains a very interesting remark about ethics.

THE "THEY"

When Dasein is absorbed in concern for the world, it is not authentically itself. Then who is it? In such cases Dasein is not itself, but rather "the they," a concept already known to us from the early Freiburg period. For instance: "They say the war will be over soon." Here, no one takes responsibility for the views of the they, and in fact it is impossible for anyone to take such responsibility. The they is everyone and no one, and tranquillizes Dasein in its being-in-the-world. Heidegger follows this remark with a rather grim portrait of Dasein's existence among its fellows: Dasein is constantly worried about how it differs from other Daseins, and about whether it has lagged behind them or has somehow attained superiority. We are not always consciously aware of this distance from other Daseins, but it is always there—even in cases when we are apparently at peace with them.

The criticisms also take a political turn aimed against Heidegger's traditional nemesis: mass democracy and its infrastructure. By riding public transportation and reading newspapers, we become like the others, sinking further and further into the they. Indeed, we live under an outright dictatorship of the they: we enjoy what they enjoy, have the same views on literature that they have, and find shocking whatever they find shocking. The they even takes on a kind of police power, as the average Dasein keeps watch over everything exceptional, to make sure that it does not somehow become threatening to the tranquility of the they. Everything original and deep gets treated as something obvious and well-known. In Heidegger's words, "every secret loses its force." Anything gained by strenuous effort is converted into a superficial object of manipulation, publicity, and marketing. The they is always right, because it never gets to the heart of the matter and so never risks being wrong. Whatever happens, the they knew it all in advance. The they is never surprised by anything.

UNDERSTANDING AND STATE OF MIND

Dasein is characterized by "state of mind" as well as "understanding"—and here we already sense the temporal structure of past and future. A state of mind can also be termed a mood. Dasein is always in some mood or another, even when it seems calm and satiated. There is no escaping moods: we master one mood only by way of a countermood. A mood tells us how things are going, and indicates that we are always "thrown" into a situation to which we must respond—for this reason, Dasein is marked by what Heidegger calls *thrownness*. A mood discloses being as a whole, and is our primary mode of access to the world. For Heidegger, a mood is not something psychologically "inner" that our minds impose on the outer world. Instead, a mood is a way of being-in-the-world. Heidegger takes especial interest in bad moods, which cover up the environment in which we exist. Above all, he gives an interesting analysis of fear, which (not surprisingly) has a threefold structure: that in the face of which we fear, that which we fear about, and fear as a unified whole. When fear occurs suddenly, it is called alarm. When it is fear of something utterly unfamiliar, it is known as dread. If the fear is both sudden and unfamiliar, the proper name for it is terror. Fear also has additional minor forms such as shyness, timidity, and the tendency to be easily startled.

Along with state of mind, Dasein is characterized by understanding (the futural moment of human existence). Although Dasein is thrown into the world, there are always possibilities locked inside this thrownness: Dasein is "thrown possibility," which could easily be rephrased as "past future." Dasein is always more than it factually is, since it runs ahead of itself by projecting new possibilities on the world that is given to it. Our understanding is usually tacit or unconscious, but it can be made explicit with the help of interpretation—which understands each thing as something specific. Only for this reason can we make assertions about the way the world is. Here, for the first time, Heidegger's great book touches on the theme of language, which has so often been the *starting point* for philosophy in the past century. For Heidegger, language waits to appear until the middle of the book, since it is derivative of Dasein's wider being-in-the-world.

IDLE TALK, CURIOSITY, AND AMBIGUITY

Dasein's inauthentic being in the world can be seen as a threefold temporal structure made up of idle talk, curiosity, and ambiguity. In *idle talk*, Dasein hears something without grasping the depth of the topic, and passes the word along to other Daseins, who then pass it along still further. Superficial writing ("scribbling") and shallow reading ("skimming") take the same form. It is impossible for the reader of any book to know how much of the material was grasped by the author with firsthand insight, and how much of it is just empty cliché heard from others and passed along as intellectual gossip. As a structure of the they, idle talk thinks that it understands everything, but puts no work into seeing anything on its own.

The futural side of inauthentic Dasein is *curiosity*, which grasps nothing deeply and is perfectly satisfied by the outer contours of things, shifting from one to the next as rapidly as possible. Curiosity never comes to a rest anywhere, but is shiftless and rootless. Its purpose is to ensure that Dasein remains tranquillized, by providing it with ever-new forms of distraction.

Taken together, these two moments give us the inauthentic present, known as *ambiguity*. Ambiguity makes it impossible for Dasein to know what is real and what is not. Even the characters in Plato's dialogues are often unsure who is a Sophist and who is a philosopher, or if there is even a difference. Much that seems real turns out to be false; much that looks shallow turns out to be deep. Worst of all, every Dasein thinks itself above the they, able to guess at hidden truths of which the they is not aware. Whenever something finally happens, everyone thinks they knew it all along anyway. In fact, everyone may even be annoyed that it happened, since this deprives them of the chance to keep guessing at it cleverly before it happens. In short, Dasein is characterized by fallenness (formerly known as "ruinance"). Fallenness is a permanent state of Dasein, and cannot be removed by any cultural or technological improvements; indeed, culture and technology often only make things worse. In fallenness, we are tranquillized by the they; they make us think we are living life to the fullest, when really we are just living the way that *they* live, and not from our own potentiality for being.

CARE

The whole of Dasein's being is defined as *care*. The German word is *Sorge*, which means "care" in the sense of worries, troubles, and travails. The being of Dasein as care is revealed in *Angst*, a favorite concept of Heidegger's French existentialist admirers such as Sartre and Albert Camus. Even Angst has a temporal structure, just like fear. But while fear is a fear of specific entities (such as murderers, witches, or deadly disease), Angst has no object. What gives us Angst is not some particular thing, but rather being-in-the-world as such; we have Angst about Dasein's own potentiality for being. Whereas fear runs away from entities, Angst flees *toward* them, as a way of escaping the dread of our own being. Angst is uncanny, and the German word *Un-heimlich* indicates that it makes us feel not at home (home = *Heim*). Heidegger says that this uncanniness of Angst is the *true* state of Dasein; it is simply concealed from us most of the time.

This brings us to the concluding remarks on reality and truth that end division 1 of the book. Heidegger attacks the usual understanding of reality as presence-at-hand. All attempts to prove the reality of the world outside our minds are a waste of time. The existence of the world is fully evident in Dasein's being-in-the-world, and to attempt to prove the world's reality is to assume a separation between Dasein and the world that was never there in the first place. If we decide to "presuppose" the reality of the world or "take it on faith" these maneuvers are equally pointless, since they assume that there is a gap between Dasein and world that *ought* to be proved, if only it could be.

Heidegger's remarks on truth are equally interesting. The classical philosophical concept of truth is "adequation of the mind with its object," which means ensuring that our ideas match the way the world really is. Heidegger rejects this model for the same reason that he rejects proofs of the existence of the external world. Namely, if knowledge is seen as adequation, it implies that the world and consciousness sit side by side, present-at-hand, trying desperately to find some way to make contact. But Dasein and world are actually united, and truth arises only from Dasein's being-in-the-world. Heidegger now pushes this idea to a controversial extreme. For Heidegger, truth and falsity exist only wherever Dasein exists. Before the birth of Dasein on this planet, Newton's laws were neither true nor untrue. (At the same time, Heidegger insists that this does not make truth subjective or relative, since Dasein does not *create* the truth, but finds it in the world as soon as it is born.) This view of truth runs counter to the views of Husserl, for whom the laws of Newton, if they are valid at all, are eternally valid even in the absence of humans.

Death, Conscience, and Resoluteness

In many respects, division 2 of *Being and Time* is less polished and more repetitive than division 1. Even so, it raises important new points. Up until now, we have only encountered inauthentic Dasein. For the purposes of working out the question of being, we must show Dasein in its authentic state. Angst already gives us a taste of authenticity, since it frees us from inauthentic absorption in the world.

DEATH

But Heidegger still wants a better sense of Dasein's being as a whole. His strategy for doing this may sound almost comically literal: for Dasein's existence to become visible as a whole, we need to look for its *death*. One obvious problem is that once we die and reach completion in our lives, we will no longer be here to analyze Dasein. As it turns out, this misses the point. What we really seek is not death as an event someday in the future that kills us off, but rather the death that is with us at every moment. As soon as we are born, we are already old enough to die. The specter of death is always with us. Dasein is thrown into death as a constant possibility of its being, as revealed in Angst. It is not death itself that interests Heidegger, but being-*towards*-death, since this attitude is with us at all times even when it is concealed by our absorption in distracting curiosities. This sort of concealment is not to be blamed on weak or fearful Daseins, but stems from the fallenness of Dasein itself.

Death is not usually a shocking event: everyone already knows about it. The they interprets death as an unlucky mishap that occurs to other Daseins sometimes. The they does not hide the fact that all Daseins must die, it simply tranquillizes us by telling us not to worry about it yet. In Heidegger's words, we all realize that "one of these days we'll die too, but right now it has nothing to do with us." The they makes efforts to ensure that death is deprived of its power to shock. We console sick people by telling them not to worry, they will be better soon and will soon be tranquillized once more. The death of another Dasein is sometimes even viewed as a tactless action that one must guard against. The they deprives us of all courage for anxiety in the face of death, since it is preferred that we not think about it or discuss it at all. While the they admits that death is certain, they do not want us to be authentically certain of our own deaths. This certainty requires the courage of Angst.

CONSCIENCE

Along with Angst, another force that makes the they collapse is conscience. Conscience calls us to be guilty, and thereby frees us into responsibility for our own being-in-the-world, which can never belong to the they. The call of conscience gives no specific information, but simply calls Dasein into its own possibilities, whatever they may be. Always a phenomenologist at heart, Heidegger says that we should stick to conscience as it appears to us, rather than inventing theories about it. This means that conscience must not be explained theologically or even biologically (for example, "conscience increases the chances of survival for our genes by helping us avoid pleasurable actions that are socially dangerous and hence decrease our reproductive opportunities"). Instead, what calls us is our Dasein itself, which feels Angst over its being.

Like Angst and being-towards-death, the call of conscience strikes us as uncanny. The call says: "Guilty!" But its primary accusation against us is not lying, bank robbery, or disloyalty. Instead, conscience reminds us that we are thrown into certain specific possibilities. We are not guilty because of some sort of debt that we owe to society or to our parents; rather, indebtedness can occur only because we are already guilty, already bound to the world. The state of being guilty belongs to Dasein at all times, and is more fundamental than any explicit knowledge we might have about our guilt. Conscience does not mean weighing ourselves down with a record of guilty deeds. Instead, it means accepting the guilt that is already there simply from the fact that we are Dasein, even if we are the purest of saints. By contrast, everyday Dasein likes to tally up all its specific good and bad actions and tries to trade them off against one another, with the end result of a good or bad conscience.

RESOLUTENESS

It would be easier for Dasein if conscience had some sort of positive content, because then we could calculate exactly what our guilt is, and exactly what the remedy might be. By the same token, it would be easier if Heidegger gave us some sort of specific ethical philosophy, with a complete list of those actions that are allowed and forbidden. Heidegger gives us no such thing. What he gives us instead is the concept of *resoluteness*, which has no specific content just as conscience has none. Resolute Dasein comes to grips with its own being in the world, and does not chatter about it with the they. Resoluteness is an authentic way of being oneself; it reveals to us whatever is possible at the current moment, and gives no specific ethical advice. A Nazi storm trooper and a resistance fighter could both be perfectly "resolute," as could Christians and Muslims, or conservatives and liberals.

To summarize, Dasein is guilty at all times, not just when it does forbidden things every now and then. The call of conscience surpasses everything said by the they, surpasses all our worldly prestige or misery, and brings us face to face with our own being. Only the anticipation of death gives Dasein authentic certainty about itself. Death is a limit situation anticipated by Dasein, lurking in our midst at all times—not a specific event that will eventually happen to us on a certain day in a certain year. But Dasein's resoluteness is always muffled by the common sense of the they, and by our absorption in the entities of the world. In Angst, being-towards-death, or conscience, we reach the original form of authentic time. These authentic moments, which remain somewhat laced with inauthenticity, show us that Dasein's being lies in its care for its own existence. Dasein is both authentic and inauthentic at the same time, which makes it *historical*. The historical structure of Dasein is the major theme of the remaining sections of *Being and Time*.

Dasein's Temporality

To review, Dasein's temporality consists of mood, understanding, and the third term "falling" that unifies them. Each of these three moments has an authentic and an inauthentic side, and Heidegger invents a number of distinctions for each of these alternatives. In the case of understanding, "anticipation" is the authentic kind while the inauthentic sort is called "awaiting." The authentic manner of Dasein's relation to past is called "repetition," while the inauthentic kind is called "forgetting." As a general rule, we are being authentic if we are concerned with Dasein's own potentiality, and inauthentic if we are absorbed with the things in the world. Fear is inauthentic, since it is hypnotized or benumbed by whatever frightens it; Heidegger agrees with Aristotle's definition of fear as "a kind of depression or bewilderment." It is very different with Angst, which frees us from our absorption with things. Resolute Dasein has Angst, but not fear. Angst reveals our authentic future and our authentic past as well. It clears away all the insignificant possibilities that distract us, and frees us for an authentic repetition. In other words, it allows us to make contact with what is truly essential in our being-in-the-world.

THE TEMPORALITY OF TRANSCENDENCE

We now reach the famous section 69 of *Being and Time*, which discusses the temporality of Dasein's transcendence. Normally, Dasein is absorbed and involved with the things in its world. Dasein deals with the system of equipment as a whole, not just individual items. The self normally forgets itself in order to use equipment or take it for granted, and this forgetting happens constantly and cannot be avoided. Even if we openly encounter items of equipment, we do not do this by just looking; the visible equipment still belongs to a system of involvements with all other tools. We also discover what is unready-to-hand whenever we are surprised to find it missing.

Given that we are usually so inauthentic, it might be asked how theoretical awareness can ever happen at all. Since everydayness is immersed in countless everyday activities, theory would seem to consist in abstaining from any sort of practice. But to abstain from manipulating things is not yet theoretical awareness. The result of abstaining is really nothing better than "just looking around." Also, theory and practice are mixed together from the start: all activity has a kind of sight, while every theory is connected with numerous untheoretical practices. In general, it is not obvious where the border lies between theoretical and untheoretical activity.

We already saw that theory is marked by what Heidegger calls the as-structure. Instead of just using entities, theory views them in some explicit way: seeing them as made out of atoms, for example. In this way, theory brings something closer to us than it initially was. In order to objectify something in knowledge, we have to overlook its specific place and its specific form of readiness-to-hand by abstracting from its context. In other words, we "thematize" objects, or make them an explicit theme.

But this would be impossible if we had not already transcended the entities in the world. We must already have risen above them in advance, before forming any theory, and realized that they held more in reserve than what we saw on their surfaces. All objectifying presupposes transcendence. Indeed, the world itself presupposes Dasein: just as there would be no truth without Dasein, Heidegger says there would be no world without Dasein. Nonetheless, the relationships of meaning found between tools in the world are not a human gridwork superimposed by Dasein on a neutral set of materials. The relationships between beings are prior to any individual entities, since individual things can only arise from the total system of meaning.

HISTORIZING

Care was described as a threefold structure of death, guilt, and conscience. This is obviously a temporal structure: being-towards-death correlates with the future, guilt is enmeshed in the burden of existence that is pre-given, and conscience assumes the burden of the past by projecting its own future possibilities. But so far, Heidegger says, his analysis has focused too much on death rather than guilt. In order to do justice to both sides of the story, we must look at the "historizing" character of Dasein: Dasein always historizes, torn between the two sides of its being. But to historize does not just mean to write history books, since history involves a special kind of knowledge that occurs only in rare cases, whereas historizing happens at every moment for every Dasein. To historize simply means to exist historically, which may happen in total ignorance of all historical information. Heidegger rightly credits the philosopher Wilhelm Dilthey with major breakthroughs into the historical nature of human being. Indeed, Heidegger respects his predecessor so greatly that in *Being and Time* he makes no attempt to go beyond Dilthey's ideas, and only hopes to clarify those ideas in terms of Heidegger's own fundamental ontology.

First, we need to ask what it means when we call something "historical." When Abraham Lincoln died from the assassin's bullet, the Secretary of State Edwin Stanton supposedly said: "now he belongs to the ages." In Heideggerian terms, this statement simply means that Lincoln is no longer present-at-hand. But this is obviously not the point, since we sometimes find that we still use very old objects in our everyday lives, such as antique cars, or heirloom jewelry and pocket watches. Although the heirloom is still present-at-hand, the world to which it belongs has disappeared. In other words, it is the *world* that is primarily historical, not individual objects. The past is never entirely gone, since its possibilities remain with us in the form of a heritage. The proper way of dealing with a heritage is through repetition. To repeat means to take over some possibility as one's own.

CHOOSING YOUR HERO

To repeat means to choose one's hero. Unfortunately, many Daseins choose the they as their hero, a grim prospect indeed. I should not repeat every exact detail of my hero's life, but adopt his or her possibilities while projecting or translating them into the new world that my own Dasein now inhabits. For example, we might expect Illinois politicians to admire Lincoln as their great forerunner, but if one of them were to wear a stovepipe hat and grow a long beard, this would seem comically inauthentic, since the world in which these things are feasible stylistic traits is no longer with us. Heideggerians can be expected to admire many features of Martin Heidegger, but when they try to write in the exact style of their hero, when they read only those poets approved by Heidegger himself, and when they spend inordinate amounts of time in the Black Forest despite being foreigners, this is not a genuine repetition. It is an attempt at borrowed glory through copying the most superficial aspect of Heidegger's life instead of seeking analogous possibilities in one's own Dasein. Repetition can be made only in a moment of vision that disavows the they by anchoring oneself in a *deeper* possibility that comes from one's hero.

FATE AND DESTINY

Heidegger follows these remarks with a fascinating discussion of fate and destiny. If Dasein can be reached by the blows of fate, this is only because Dasein in its very depths *is* fate. As Nietzsche put it, accidents do not really happen: supposed "accidents" affect me differently from how they affect others, since my Dasein is a unique possibility not interchangeable with the others. Which just goes to show that they are not really accidents at all. For Heidegger it is only irresolute people, driven in random directions by chance events, who fail to come to grips with their fate. The corresponding term, when dealing with multiple Daseins who historize together, is destiny. The German, Russian, and American peoples all have a destiny, different in each case, and this destiny is not built by piecing together all the fates of the individual people in these nations. Rather, the destiny of a people already contains the fate of the individuals within it. But it is not only nations that have a destiny: generations have destinies as well. Dasein already recognizes this when it gives them special nicknames: the lost generation, the greatest generation, the baby boom, Generation X. By the same token, it is not just people who have fates. Books, buildings, universities, and even grandfather clocks and diamond rings have fates of their own.

Inauthentic historizing makes us forget the fate of our Dasein and everything else, in favor of whatever happens to be present-at-hand. Like all forms of knowledge, history is not something completely neutral and free, but swells up from the historian's own historical existence. It is not just some sort of lamentable bias if British, French, Austrian, and Turkish histories of World War I differ in their tone and conclusions, since there is no such thing as a present-at-hand World War I in itself, viewed from nowhere.

PUBLIC TIME

Time is always datable, and can be measured on a clock or calendar whenever we please. This is because time is public, and public time arises only from the more original time of Dasein itself. In this connection Heidegger often speaks of clock-time or world-time. Clock-time is a present-at-hand series of "nows" that completely overlooks the fundamental threefold structure of Dasein's temporality. This is pleasing to the they, which does not want to face guilt, conscience, or death. The they does not die, because it cannot. The they assumes no guilt, and hears no call of conscience, because it is tranquillized and wishes to tranquillize everyone.

On this note, we reach the end of Heidegger's great book. He ends by humbly declaring that the book is merely provisional, and by asking a series of further questions. *Being and Time* was a beloved work from the start, immediately recognized as a landmark event in philosophy. There are at least two reasons for this. First, Heidegger seemed to bring the great question of ancient Greek philosophy back to life: what is the meaning of being? Unlike the schoolmasters of his era who filled philosophy textbooks with secondhand theories drawn from dead thinkers, Heidegger seemed to be repeating the original drama of ancient Greek thought. His sincerity was contagious, and won him many admirers among his students and readers, despite his often prickly personality.

Second, and perhaps even more importantly, *Being and Time* seemed to bring the actual lives of human beings into philosophy, rather than excluding them as something lying outside rigorous thought. As one early admirer of the book put it, before Heidegger it used to be that students entered the lecture hall and had to force themselves into "philosophy mode": using artificial technical terms and dealing with problems in a preapproved academic way. After the lecture, students would leave the university, smoke cigarettes, become absorbed in newspapers and public transportation, experience fear, Angst, or guilt, and deal with all manner of personal problems. But all of this was just everyday life, not an acceptable topic of philosophy. It was Heidegger who changed this (though Husserl deserves some of the credit as well). In Heidegger's wake, even our most trivial moments of gossip or shyness become central themes of philosophy. This had immediate appeal to many readers in Heidegger's time, and gave him an ever-increasing following as he struck new roots at the University of Freiburg.

5

Freiburg before the Rectorate

Although Heidegger was still a young man in 1928, his greatest book was already behind him. The years from 1928 to 1932 saw him at the pinnacle of his reputation, holding an important university chair and drawing to Freiburg some of the best students he would ever have. The future must have looked uniformly bright at this point. Heidegger would be remembered very differently if he had unexpectedly died some time during this period. Although we would have lost a great deal of additional philosophy from such a premature death, it seems likely that a hypothetical obituary writer in 1930 would have expected even greater writings than were ever produced.

More specifically, I would suggest that Heidegger's development began to stall in exactly 1930. "What is Metaphysics?" the lecture on nothingness delivered in 1929, still shows Heidegger at his most energetic, pressing toward new insights in inventive language. The 1929–30 lecture course on boredom and animal life was perhaps the boldest effort of his career, and even the ultimate failure of the course fails to erase the pleasant aftertaste of these lectures. Somewhat controversially, I would point to 1930 as the beginning of a narrowing of Heidegger's vision. The famous essay from that year on "truth," which is discussed in this chapter due to its great influence, is in my view heavily overrated. After the daring attempt to grasp the essence of animal life, we are now left with a somewhat abstract play of veiling and unveiling, absence and presence. The great fertility of the Marburg period begins to fade, and Heidegger becomes steadily bogged down in his past triumphs until finally securing a new mature orientation much later, after the war. Readers are advised that this is by no means the universal opinion: the Heidegger of the 1930s has numerous rabid fans. I wish them well, but cannot follow them.

I would also suggest that the growing staleness beginning in 1930 had severe biographical consequences—for it is difficult to imagine the Martin Heidegger of 1925 or 1926 volunteering to commit his time to serving as rector of the University of Freiburg. Even great thinkers experience fatigue after their discoveries. There is reason to believe that the intellectual fatigue of the early 1930s was one of the primary sources for Heidegger's sudden administrative and political enthusiasms, areas in which he was so obviously lacking in talent and good judgment.

1929: Nothingness

Although Heidegger's return to Freiburg came in 1928, his inaugural lecture was given the following year. This was the famous "What Is Metaphysics?" Regarded by many readers as a deeply inspiring work, it was also denounced as sheer nonsense by the philosopher Rudolf Carnap, who believed that most philosophical problems are caused by the sloppy use of language. The topic of Heidegger's lecture is nothingness, and it is easy enough to imagine why Carnap sees no way to discuss "nothing" as a real concept.

THREEFOLD KNOWLEDGE

As was often the case during his career, Heidegger begins his lecture by asking about the character of science, in the broad sense of systematic knowledge. We who teach and study in the universities are occupied with knowledge, and knowledge has a threefold structure (such a surprise!). Here as always, Heidegger is able to coin yet another new trio of terms to describe his recurrent model of temporality. First, science is *related to the world*, which we can identify with Heidegger's "past," since the world is that which is already given to us. Second, science always has some specific *attitude*. This can be identified with Heidegger's "future," since attitude means that there are many different ways to project the world that is given to us. The third and unifying term is *Einbruch*, which in German can mean a break-in or burglary, but in this context is sometimes translated as "irruption," for lack of a better term—a kind of violent entrance into a place. Dasein is always thrown into a relation with the world and approaches this world with a specific attitude, and the unity of these two terms defines the nature of science.

NOTHINGNESS

Heidegger's next step might seem like a word trick. Namely, he tells us that the common link between world-relationship, attitude, and irruption is that all are concerned with the things with which they are concerned—and outside of that, *nothing*. Hence, a true understanding of science would require an understanding of what we mean by nothing. But this is not a simple word trick, since what Heidegger points to here is the concept of finitude. If everything is what it is and nothing more, this implies that there is something beyond each thing: something that it is not. For Heidegger, this makes nothingness not just a legitimate theme of philosophy, but a pivotal one, since philosophy must always deal with the finitude of the world and the things within it. By contrast, science never deals with nothing, but always with this or that specific thing: flowers, asteroids, glaciers. As Heidegger puts it, science wishes to know nothing about nothing.

It might seem to some readers that there is no such thing as nothing—after all, nothing *is* nothing, and hence in a way it is actually something. For other readers, nothingness might seem to be little more than a grammatical illusion resulting from our use of the word "not." But Heidegger insists that the nothingness he describes is deeper than all negation and all logic. As he puts it, nothingness is the negation of the totality of beings, and this must be achieved in a special way. We cannot just form an idea of beings as a whole and then imagine ourselves drawing a red "X" through them to negate all these beings. This would merely give us an external *concept* of nothingness, not nothingness itself.

ANGST

There is a big difference between having a concept of beings as a whole and actually finding oneself in the midst of this whole. The way we find ourselves in the midst of beings is through certain fundamental moods that make the whole real for us. We confront beings as whole in boredom, a mood that Heidegger will soon spend half a semester describing in detail. We also confront the whole when we are in the presence of the Dasein of a beloved person. Yet these moods immerse us in the whole and cause us to be fascinated with it. In this way, they actually conceal nothingness from us. The experience of nothingness comes from the fundamental mood of Angst, already described in detail in *Being and Time*. By contrast, we do not encounter nothingness in the moods of anxiousness or fear: these moods are always fearfully absorbed in specific threats, and for this reason they miss the nothing completely. In Angst, everything sinks into a sort of indifference that lies beyond our grasp. Reality does not disappear, but presses upon us all the more. Angst places us into a kind of hovering or suspension (as far back as 1919, Heidegger had said that all theoretical behavior does this). Angst neither grasps nothingness in conceptual terms, nor views it as some sort of object. We remain calm in the mood of Angst, despite its sheer uncanniness. We shrink back, but do not flee.

Beings as Such and as a Whole

In this way, nothingness "nihilates" the world, confronting us with beings as a whole. "The nothing nothings," as Heidegger famously puts it. Angst brings Dasein before beings *as a whole*, but also before beings *as such*. It is worth pausing briefly to discuss this distinction between "as a whole" and "as such." It recurs frequently in the later years of Heidegger's career, especially in his interpretation of Nietzsche, and has received too little attention from scholars. At various moments, Heidegger tells us that these terms are the heirs of the classical distinction between existence (beings as a whole) and essence (beings as such). Beings as a whole refers to the existence shared by all things, whereas beings as such refers to the specific nature of each being that makes it what it is. Heidegger accepts this distinction, even though he rejects the traditional split between existence and essence, which he thinks reduces things to presence. Both moments are present in everything that exists, at all times. Beings as a whole and beings as such can both be revealed to us, as happens in Angst. But even when we do not experience Angst, beings as a whole and as such are still there, lying in concealment. No thing could exist without both of these sides: everything that is both exists, and exists as a certain specific thing.

While most of Heidegger's philosophy is dominated by endless repetitions of a single recurrent duel between concealed and revealed, sheltering and clearing, tool and broken tool, or past and future (these pairs are all the same), the difference between beings as such and beings as a whole plays out on *both* sides of this distinction: the realms of shadow and of visibility. This means that the difference between "as a whole" and "as such" cuts across Heidegger's more prominent first dualism. In 1949 at the very latest, Heidegger will draw the conclusion that these two dualisms split the world into quadrants, and he will give us the model of a fourfold universe.

ANGST AND TRANSCENDENCE

It is the essence of Dasein to be held out into nothingness. After all, Dasein must partly transcend the world, or it would never be able to develop theories about the world. It rises above entities because it sees them as finite, and is able to grasp their contours. Since being and beings are both always finite, being and beings alike must exist against the background of nothingness that we find in Angst. It might seem strange to grant such an important role to Angst, since even Heidegger admits that this mood is so rare that it strikes most people only a few times in their lives. In one sense this is true. But in another sense, Heidegger thinks that Angst is not rare at all, but is with us constantly without our knowing it. We hover in Angst at every moment, but most of the time it "sleeps." We allow it to remain asleep through our obsession with specific objects. Like all other fundamental moods, Angst can either be awake or asleep, but in either case it is always present.

Angst can awaken at any moment, since it is not caused by any specific sadness or disappointment; in fact, Heidegger says that it has a certain relation to cheerfulness and the sense of longing. Humans are the placeholders or hearth-keepers of nothingness. Only because Dasein constantly hovers in the nothing, transcending the things of the world, are we able to ask "why?" about anything. And since we constantly transcend the world, there is a sense in which we are always asking "why?" even in moments of superficiality and outright stupidity. The question "why?" is simply sleeping, and needs to be awakened by a fundamental mood. In this respect, philosophy belongs to the essence of being human. All humans are philosophers, but in most of them, philosophy is sleeping rather than awake. Without this deeper form of nothingness, there could be no negation using the word "not," since everything we encounter would seem infinite and unsurpassable if not for Dasein's transcendence of the world.

This implies that logic is only a secondary part of philosophy, not the primary part as Carnap believes. For Heidegger, all logic is swept away by the whirlwind of a more original form of questioning, which we might call metaphysics (in the good sense of the term). The deepest question that humans can ask is "why is there something rather than nothing?" There is no real answer to this question, since Heidegger will not be satisfied with any causal explanation of how God or the Big Bang created the universe. The question is not meant to be answered, but is designed to awaken the fundamental mood of Angst. A few months after delivering this lecture, Heidegger was focused on a different but related mood: boredom.

1929–30: On Boredom and Animals

The 1929–30 Freiburg lecture course is one of Heidegger's most popular, and certainly one of his most interesting. The title of the course is *Fundamental Concepts of Metaphysics: World, Finitude, Solitude.* As usual, the trio of words in the subtitle reflects the triple structure of temporality. In this course, Heidegger works out the structure of temporality through a fascinating analysis of three increasingly deep forms of boredom. He then returns to a closer examination of the first key term: world.

ANIMALS ARE POOR IN WORLD

While a stone is worldless and a human being has world, animals are said to be *poor* in world. Animals present a key problem for Heidegger that he never quite manages to solve. René Descartes, the first modern philosopher, took perhaps the most extreme position on animals ever known. Since animals cannot be said to be thinking substance as humans are, Descartes concludes that they are sheer physical machines—so that screams of pain from a monkey are no better than the squeaking gears of a machine that has not been properly oiled. Heidegger realizes that this view is unconvincing. Even so, he faces a serious problem in trying to explain animal life in his own terms. His entire philosophy revolves around the distinction between the being of objects such as chairs or trees, and their explicit presence to humans "as" chairs or trees. In one sense, to be able to perceive anything at all seems to require an as-structure: after all, if moths and rabbits could not see things *as* things, everything would recede into darkness and animals would perceive nothing at all. In another way, however, only human Dasein possesses the "as" in the truest sense, given that only humans can ask explicit questions about beings or about being itself.

Heidegger's new concept of "world-poverty" is his attempt to explain the strange special case of animals. Animals are not world-less, but poor in world. Yet it should be noted that Heidegger has nothing to say in these lectures about reproduction, nutrition, locomotion, or other well-known features of living creatures. He tries to approach the human/animal divide solely through examining the distinct forms of the "as" in human and animal perception. For this reason, he has nothing at all to say about plants or fungi, which presumably do not perceive the world in the way that animals do. The 1929–30 course is probably the high-water mark of Heidegger's efforts to develop the "metontology" mentioned earlier—a philosophy able to come to grips with *specific* forms of reality. Following the failure of this course (admittedly a mesmerizing failure), he never attempted such a thing again. For the remainder of his career, he would deal with the as-structure only by retreating into a somewhat abstract discussion of the interplay between light and shadow, although it was later expanded into an intriguing fourfold structure, as we will see.

BOREDOM

Viewed from the outside, philosophy might be confused with science or with the creation of a world-view. Heidegger holds that it is neither of these things. But this frequent confusion is no accident, and signals the deep-seated *ambiguity* of philosophy, which has a disturbingly close relation to superficiality and sophistry. One can only grows ripe for philosophy with one's entire Dasein, which is why seventeen-year-olds are able to make great discoveries in mathematics but not in philosophy. Philosophers always stand on the verge of error, since they try to listen into the depths of things without ever fully hearing those depths. This makes philosophy a turbulent vocation, divorced from the search for comfort. We do not begin to philosophize by reading great books of the past or dreaming up brilliant arguments against our opponents. Instead, we must awaken in ourselves a fundamental mood that grips all human Dasein from time to time, but which grips philosophers to an especial degree. In the 1929–30 course, Heidegger selects the fundamental mood of boredom, which should be familiar enough to everyone. He describes boredom in three increasingly intense forms, and in doing so gives us perhaps the best phenomenological descriptions he ever made.

BOREDOM, LEVEL ONE

For the first form of boredom, Heidegger asks us to imagine that we have arrived too early for our train at a dull provincial station of some minor regional railway. We learn that there are still four hours until the train arrives. We have a book with us, but cannot read it; we have some thoughts worth developing, but cannot get a grip on them. Instead, we go outside and count the trees, pace back and forth along the platform, scan the timetables aimlessly, and look at our watches again and again. What bores us here is not the simple act of waiting, since waiting sometimes involves excitement or suspense. What bores us is that we are forced to drive away the time. We cannot escape, but are *held in limbo* by the boring situation, as time drags along. The things around us leave us numb. They do not disappear, since we remain attached to them—yet they somehow *leave us empty*. In this boring situation, we are abandoned to ourselves. The station bores us because we are unable simply to use it as a station, but are forced to linger there. It may be our own fault for having misread the schedule, or maybe the railway company ineptly mismanaged its traffic. But all blame is beside the point: however it happened, we are now stuck in this boring station, trying to drive away the time.

In this first form of boredom, we are held in limbo to the station while also being left empty through our inability to make use of it. This links up with the term *world* from the subtitle, for it is the world that bores us here—a system of interrelated things whose emptiness holds us in limbo.

BOREDOM, LEVEL TWO

The second form of boredom is even more profound, according to Heidegger. Imagine that you are invited to a small dinner party. There is no need to go, but also no reason to avoid it; you accept the invitation, put your work aside for the night, and make your way to the dinner. There turns out to be nothing wrong with the evening. Everyone is elegant and friendly. The food is tasty, cigars are smoked, and the entire experience is not unpleasant. But returning home after polite farewells, you realize: "I was truly bored this evening." This case of boredom is clearly different from that of the train station. It is not the things or people at the dinner that bored you, because there was nothing the least bit wrong with any of them. Here too, you were held in limbo and left empty, but not in the same way as before. What happened is that you left your proper self at home this evening, and this is what left you empty. It was an emptiness of *yourself*, not of the things or people at the party. You were held in limbo because you were not truly present at the party, and for this reason were abandoned to your empty self. You were trapped completely in the present, out of touch with your potentiality or projects for being in the world. What bored you in this case was not the world, but rather the *solitude* of your Dasein, another of the three key terms in Heidegger's subtitle. Heidegger sees this sort of boredom as especially relevant to the modern world, in which everyone tries to become involved with everything, leaving no one with enough time for anything. Everyone is too busy for anything essential.

BOREDOM, LEVEL THREE

The third form of boredom is the deepest of them all. Heidegger describes this situation with the phrase: "one is bored." For example, we can imagine walking through the streets of a large city on a Sunday afternoon (far more boring in Europe than in the United States). Nothing is open, and the sidewalks are empty; no possibilities exist for distraction. Everything is shrouded in a profound emptiness that we are forced to confront, unlike the other two cases where we could try to drive away the time or sink into empty pleasures. On this Sunday afternoon, beings as a whole refuse themselves to us. This is not the same sort of nothingness experienced in Angst, because the boring city continues to overpower us with its absolute presence. We are left in the lurch, held in limbo by beings as a whole. But in this way, we do manage to make contact with something essential: namely, we are explicitly confronted with our own Dasein, its possibilities, and our thrownness into the world. We are entranced by time, unable to escape it. This form of boredom is linked to the third key term from the subtitle, *finitude*, since it confronts us with the total situation of our Dasein in the world.

We can now review all three forms of boredom. The train station gives us boredom with the world, which corresponds to the moment of *past*—since it is the things in which we are already immersed in the station that leave us empty. The dinner party gives us boredom with our own being, which corresponds to the moment of *future*—since it is Dasein's own projection of its possibilities that is emptied of significance. But the boring city on Sunday gives us boredom with beings as a whole, which corresponds to the unified moment of *present*—since it is the entire unified structure of being-in-the-world that leaves us empty here. In a sense, being itself is boring.

The best escape from this boredom, Heidegger says, would be through a sense of danger. He asks us, in the manner of a challenge, whether we have enough courage to embrace such danger. This would require a moment of vision that ruptures the emptiness of being as a whole. What we really need is someone capable of inspiring our Dasein with *terror* again. Heidegger is not optimistic about this, since even World War I did not give sufficient terror to our Dasein. But a few names in recent history immediately come to mind as impeccable sources of terror, and there would be no need for Heidegger to wait long for their arrival.

TOOLS AND ORGANS

Heidegger now turns to a closer examination of world, more specifically to the problem of animals being "poor" in world. Obviously, animals must have some access to the world, but not in the way that Dasein does: dogs "live," but they do not "exist" as Dasein does. Animals have world but also do not have it, which makes animals the central problem of Heidegger's lecture course. But before drawing distinctions between humans and animals, he zeroes in on a feature shared by both. Humans and animals are both living organisms, which means that both have bodily organs. For this reason, it is important to show the difference between organs and tools.

Hammers, buses, and windows are ready-to-hand. Each of them is assigned to a particular system of objects, and each disappears into this system as long as it fulfills its purpose. Tools are serviceable, at least until they break. But the handiness of tools is not the same as the *capacity* of organs. Or more precisely, it is the organism as a whole that has capacities, not the organ, since a bodily organ detached from its body is not an organ at all. Here, Heidegger agrees with Aristotle's remark that what hears, smells, and tastes is the soul (whatever it may be), not the ears, nose, or tongue. Tools are serviceable, in the sense that we can grab any pen off any table and use it. This is not true of organs: we need our own eyes and ears to sense anything. If we someday receive an organ transplant, this simply means that we are making the new organ our own. Organs are not serviceable for the organism, but *subservient* to it. What makes the organs subservient is that they arise from a capacity lying in the organism itself. As Heidegger puts it, the potential for seeing is what makes the eye, not vice versa. After all, an eyeball created by random mutation would just sit around as useless dead weight if the rest of the organism were not already open to outside influence by light. Heidegger cites the example of an amoeba, which is able to form and reabsorb its own organs on the spur of the moment in response to specific needs. An amoeba is able to do this because the capacity comes from the amoeba itself, and the organs are improvised to fit that capacity. Organs are not present-at-hand pieces of physical material, but neither are they ready-to-hand items of equipment. Instead, organs exist only in life. There is an inner drive in the organism, unlike in hammers, which have no urge to do their hammering. Tools can be destroyed, but they can never atrophy: that is to say, a tool either works or fails to work, whereas an organ can either develop or decay, thereby increasing or reducing the capacity of the organism by degrees. Animal organisms can be viewed as a kind of instinctual self-driving. Animal behavior is marked by instinct or drive because animals are captivated by the world. By contrast, human comportment is characterized by action.

This brings us to the central question of the difference between humans and animals. Heidegger admits that he is unable to give a complete description of animal life in this lecture course. His limited focus is on the as-structure, which belongs only to human Dasein. What he does give us is a full description of animal "captivation," illuminated by a series of fascinating (though cruel) experiments with bees. In these experiments, bees are thrown into confusion by having their hives moved several meters away during their absence; they are trapped for several hours in a box, lose their orientation as the sun changes position, and become lost on the way home; they have their abdomens sliced away by researchers as they are sucking honey, and continue sucking honey until they die. All these examples are meant to suggest that animal behavior is not open to beings as such. Beings are neither manifest to animals nor closed off to them. There is no as-structure in animal behavior, no "letting-be" of entities. Animals are bound to their environment.

Heidegger reached this model of animals by beginning with the human essence and disassembling it piece by piece. This human essence is described by Heidegger as world-forming. Humans are not just captivated by the world, but comport themselves toward it. Dasein lives in the as-structure and is able to see beings as beings. This is what establishes that human beings have world, for world means nothing other than the accessibility of beings. In this context, Heidegger reminds us of his early favorite term, formal indication. What philosophy should really be trying to do is hint or point toward the depths of the world, since all clear and explicit statements have the tendency to convert everything into presence-at-hand, and this is what must be avoided. Dasein is world-forming because, unlike animals, it projects a world. Following the usual rhythm of Heidegger's books, this projection has a threefold structure: Dasein brings world forth, gives an image or view of the world, and constitutes the world. This sort of temporality is lacking in the case of animal life.

The 1929–30 course, engrossing though it is, can only be regarded as a failure. Heidegger is unable to resolve the crucial problem with the as-structure: it is supposed to hold good for all perception whatsoever, but at the same time is also supposed to explain the superiority of theoretical awareness over simple perception. His attempts to distinguish between human and animal reality never really solidify. Further evidence for this comes from the fact that Heidegger never published his findings from this course. Nor did he develop the theme further in later lecture courses. The 1929–30 course was a strange, isolated attempt to break fresh ground. While it is not Heidegger's second master-work, it is surely his most interesting dead end.

1930: Veiling and Unveiling

During the 1930s, Heidegger began to show increasing interest in the concept of *truth*. The celebrated essay "On the Essence of Truth" is the beginning of this phase of his career, although there were numerous precursors in *Being and Time* and even earlier. What Heidegger always opposes is the traditional concept of truth as adequation between mind and reality. According to this model, a real world sits outside the human mind, and the mind is correct when its ideas about the world match the way the world really is. In this model, there are things present-at-hand in the world, ideas present-at-hand in the mind, and the goal is to correlate the ideas with the things. From our discussion of *Being and Time*, you may be able to guess that Heidegger will oppose the model of truth as adequation and offer a competing account.

First, he attacks the idea of an isolated mind trying to corre-spond with an isolated world, since Dasein is always being-in-the-world, which means that world and Dasein are inseparable. Second, he attacks the idea that truth means correctness by show-ing that Dasein's view of the world is never really correct or incor-rect. Instead, Dasein *unveils* the truth, and this implies numerous possible levels of understanding, each of them a specific mixture of light and shadow. Dasein exists in the world, and uncovers the world. Neither of these features of Dasein allow for adequation as a successful model of truth.

OPENNESS

In the course of life we encounter various things and statements: true, false, profound, superficial, or some mixture of all of these. The things we deal with are encountered explicitly *as such*: we do not deal with shapeless lumps, but with dogs, flames, weapons, and stars. To deal with such things requires an open space. No aware-ness of things is possible unless we and they stand in an open space of encounter where both reside. Any correctness or incorrectness is possible only on the basis of such an openness. Hence, this openness is what deserves to be called truth in the essential sense. This gives us a preliminary solution to the "essence of truth" described in the title: the essence of truth is openness. Since openness requires freedom, we can also say that the essence of truth is freedom. While freedom is usually regarded as a property belonging to humans, Heidegger holds that the reverse is true: humans are the property of freedom. Without freedom, we would not be Dasein. To be free means to be exposed to the unconcealment of beings. Any logical truth of sentences is shallow in comparison with this deeper revelation of things in human freedom. The essence of truth is letting things be, so that they can appear to us as what they really are, without our violently reducing them to distortions or caricatures. Naturally, such distortion is always partly unavoidable.

UNCONCEALMENT

The openness of Dasein and things requires unconcealment. The Greek name for unconcealment is *aletheia*, which means drawing something forgotten into visibility. For Heidegger this is a uniquely human gift, and human burden. Most entities just sit around in the world, present-at-hand, aware of nothing. But human Dasein, unlike trees or cement blocks, is held out amidst beings as they conceal and reveal themselves. When the first human silently wondered what beings are, this was the first moment of unconcealment, and the true beginning of history. Since humans are the ones who exist outside themselves in the world, it is only humans who are immersed in the play of absence and presence that unfolds in the course of history. Nature itself has no history, even though numerous astronomical or geological events occur. The rare and simple decisions of history are based on the way that the essence of truth comes to presence. Because of the two-sided nature of this process, beings are always partly concealed. Illusion or semblance often dominates, and some things may remain concealed for centuries. We cannot understand truth unless we also understand untruth, since they are two sides of the same coin. Untruth does not simply refer to errors or mistakes in the usual sense, but to a deeper level of error inherent in reality itself.

ERRANCE

But concealment is not just something that robs or deprives us of beings—it also preserves what is proper to the things. It not only withholds reality from us, but shelters it and lets it be, deeper than the thin facades through which they become visible to us. Concealment guards what is secret. Yet the concealment itself can also be forgotten, leading us to focus entirely on what becomes present. Dasein becomes mired in what is customary, because Dasein is insistent no less than existent: it stands inside itself no less than outside. Humans are constantly torn between the secret and that which is accessible. This double interplay can be called errance; all human life is errance. More than this, being itself is errance, since the essence of truth must always be shadowed by a "counteressence." To point toward the secret even as it withdraws is the original essence of philosophy. This later became metaphysics in the bad sense, by giving priority to the special status of one kind of entity as the cause or ground of all others. Likewise, philosophy also reverses into sophistry, or the dominance of the commonsense understanding. It would not be too extreme to say that philosophy is always mixed with bad metaphysics and with sophistry. Like everything else in the world, philosophy is ambiguous. Its essence is always accompanied by a counteressence that makes it appear in a sham form as semblance.

Even the fundamental mood required for philosophy is ambiguous. In one sense, philosophy needs an attitude of releasement or gentleness that lets things simply be what they are. But in another sense, philosophy requires the resoluteness of strength, which projects upon things in its own forceful way. When philosophy lets things be, this is not just an opening, but also a concealment. The proper relation to concealment is always *tact*. Having a sense of tact is often more important than having an abundance of knowledge. Tact cannot be taught, since it amounts to having the right touch or feel for a specific subject matter.

The essence of truth is nothing human. Essence shows itself, which means that being shows itself. Heidegger now switches to an older German spelling of the word for being: from *Sein* to *Seyn*. We can ignore this change for the remainder of the book, since all options for translating it are equally clumsy. But just this once, we can say that "beyng" is the difference that prevails between being and beings. The basic characteristic of beyng is its truth—which both shelters and clears. From now on, Heidegger believes, thinking must concern itself with this interplay of shadow and light. In so doing, thinking does not just give us concepts and representations, but changes our very relation to being. With this step we overcome bad metaphysics, which misses the play of absence and presence and sets up the sheer dominance of presence. When this happens, there will be a turn within the history of being itself.

In the midst of Heidegger's reflections on the turn in the history of being, there was an abrupt turn in the history of Germany. In following the call of this turn, Heidegger gave us the most infamous moment not only of his own career, but of the history of philosophy as a whole.

6

A Nazi Philosopher

Reports from Heidegger's acquaintances suggest that he already supported National Socialism in the early 1930s, well before it showed its ugliest face to the world. As Heidegger sometimes mentioned in his own defense, there was a difference between supporting Hitler in 1930, 1936, or 1942. This may be so. But in Heidegger's breakthrough year of 1919, his fellow twenty-nine-year-old Adolf Hitler had a "breakthrough" of his own. The eventual Führer concluded that the final goal of anti-Semitism must be the complete removal of the Jews. In 1924, as Heidegger began his sparkling half-decade in Marburg, Hitler wrote in *Mein Kampf* that the Jew is a parasite on the German nation. He hinted darkly that at least some Jews should be put out of their misery with poison gas, and asserted that this was a question of life and death for Germany—a question not for the faint of heart. Although Heidegger claimed never to have read *Mein Kampf*, it seems fair to say that he has some explaining to do.

When Heidegger finally became Husserl's assistant in 1918, he replaced a talented and somewhat younger Jewish woman named Edith Stein, who had tired of the assistantship. A few years later, Stein had a deep religious experience while reading the *Autobiography* of St. Teresa of Avila, and converted to Roman Catholicism. Forced from her teaching position by the Nazis in 1933, she entered a convent under the name Teresa Benedicta of the Cross. The Church later transferred her to Holland, away from the persecutions unfolding in Germany. But the Nazis saw nothing holy in Teresa Benedicta: in 1942, she was arrested by German occupation forces in the Netherlands and shipped to Auschwitz.

There she was gassed to death, just as Hitler's book had proposed. She was raised to sainthood in 1998. The ashes of this saint lie with those of millions of others destroyed in the Birkenau camp.

Emmanuel Levinas was a gifted Lithuanian Jew who came to Freiburg to study with Husserl, but fell under Heidegger's spell instead. *Being and Time* worked its magic on Levinas like few other readers, and he remains one of the most profound readers of Heidegger we have. As a member of the French Army, Levinas was captured early in the German invasion of 1940, and spent the remainder of the war in a prisoner camp near Hanover. Spared the death camps by the Geneva Convention, he was nonetheless forced to wear a Star of David and live in cramped quarters, and wrote his greatest pages on Heidegger during short breaks from forced labor. Even so, he was luckier than his family members, as he was horrified to learn after the war. In his hometown of Kaunas, an SS soldier had shot his immediate family to death. In France, his mother-in-law was deported and never heard from again. The same thing nearly happened to his wife, who was saved only through the efforts of the philosopher Maurice Blanchot.

Paul Celan, one of the most celebrated poets of the twentieth century, was born a Romanian Jew at the unluckiest possible moment in history. Young Celan was sent into forced labor by the Nazis, and his parents were slaughtered. He later became an admirer of Heidegger's philosophy and even wrote a poem about the philosopher's Black Forest hut. Celan and Heidegger eventually got to know one another, and Celan was understandably conflicted, at first refusing to meet Heidegger at all, then getting to know him, only to withdraw angrily once again. Heidegger eventually decided that Celan was a hopeless case. Perhaps Heidegger was right: on May 1, 1970, the anguished Celan drowned himself in the River Seine in Paris.

Of the millions whose lives were shattered by the movement that Heidegger supported, I have mentioned only a few who can be linked to him personally. It is only fair that we not forget Edith Stein and the family members of Levinas and Celan as we listen to Heidegger giving his rectoral address in 1933, with Nazi pep music ringing in the air. It is also fair that we not exaggerate the philosopher's own role in the crimes of the Third Reich. His most unsavory deeds as university rector will be described below. But there are good reasons why Heidegger merely lost his professorship after the war, rather than being imprisoned or hanged. The political philosopher Carl Schmitt (now greatly in fashion) was far more compromised, and spent months under arrest by the Allies. Alfred Rosenberg, a high Nazi official and author of openly racist philosophical works, was executed at Nuremberg in 1946. The occupying powers were obviously right not to place Heidegger in the same category. The final Allied verdict on the philosopher was "fellow traveler." Though not one of the hardcore Nazi intellectuals, he was a loyal party member nonetheless, and someone who had given substantial moral comfort to the movement.

1933: The Rectoral Address

It has justly been remarked that Heidegger's infamous rectoral address is not just a piece of hack political propaganda. While it is certainly his most disturbing piece of work, "The Self-Assertion of the German University" is a genuine philosophical speculation, and deserves to be treated as such. The address was delivered in an atmosphere of outright Fascist carnival. The date was May 27, 1933. Heidegger had been elected rector of the University in April, and on May 1 he officially joined the Nazi Party. He thereupon fired off pompous "Sieg Heil!" messages to various colleagues, and even invited Carl Schmitt to join the Nazi Party (Schmitt had already done so). On May 23, Heidegger announced plans for his inauguration ceremony four days later. First would come the playing of the "Horst Wessel Song," the Nazi anthem in honor of a stock party hero, a young street thug killed in a brawl in Berlin. "Sieg Heil!" would then be shouted, with right arms raised in the Nazi salute.

Surely, no major philosophical lecture has been delivered under such unsettling circumstances, which would be laughable if not for the brutal successes of the movement. The rectoral address is just under ten pages long in the original German, and is surely the most infamous document in the history of philosophy. But although the Nazi anthems and chanted slogans and decorative swastikas surrounding the lecture may astonish the readers of this book, the words of Heidegger's address will not. "The Self-Assertion of the German University" fits perfectly in the train of his philosophical development.

By becoming rector, Heidegger says, he assumes spiritual leadership of the University. But leaders themselves must also be led, and what they must follow is the spiritual task presented by the destiny of the German people. While most people emphasize the self-*administration* of universities, Heidegger says that administration requires that we know ourselves, and this demands self-*reflection*. Self-reflection, in turn, happens only through self-*assertion*, which we can either achieve or fail to achieve. Here, the familiar threefold structure of temporality returns in a new, politicized context. If not for all the Nazi music and Hitler salutes, nothing here would surprise readers of Heidegger's earlier writings.

The self-assertion of the university involves a kind of group authenticity, to use the language of *Being and Time*. Now as in 1919, Heidegger tells us that only *science* (in the broadest sense of all systematic knowledge) allows us to reach our true foundations. Repeating his usual threefold structure, Heidegger says that science (projection or futuricity) must go hand in hand with German destiny (thrownness or past) if the German university is to reach its essence (present). Yet there is no way of touching our destiny unless we make contact with the power of the Greek beginning. Greek philosophy is the place where humans first take a stand amidst beings as a whole, interrogating and grasping them.

But not only do we stand under the obligation of the Greek beginning as our destiny, Heidegger continues. To an equal degree, we must also step out into the open by questioning. (The familiar interplay of thrownness and projection is obvious here.) Questioning unlocks what is essential in all things. It forces us into the most extreme simplification of our destiny, and eliminates all the mindless scattering of the university into various professional disciplines. If we wish to pursue such radical questioning, we should realize that it exposes us to the most intimate and most extreme danger, which comes only in the world of the spirit (and Heidegger does not mean religion). The spiritual world of a people is what guarantees a people its greatness. The German people has already begun its march toward this future, and has already chosen greatness over degeneration and decay. Teachers are obliged to press forward to the most extreme posts of danger. But this requires the courage for solitude: what is most decisive in leadership is often the ability to walk alone.

There is no need to wake the German students from their slumber, since they are already on the march. They seek leaders. The German word here is *Führer*, and Hitler is one of the leaders Heidegger had in mind, along with himself. The students are willing to stand firm in three distinct kinds of service (by now, the number three should never come as a surprise). There is work service, defense service, and service in knowledge, all of them equally important. These three are unified by *being*, which is the one thing most worthy of questioning.

Here we find a strange mixture of Nazi politics with the philosophical revolution of *Being and Time*, as if Hitler were showing the same openness to being in the political realm that Heidegger had attained in philosophy. Everyone will agree that this was a naive interpretation of Nazi motives. But for Rector Heidegger, the unity of all professions and disciplines under the aegis of being has clear practical consequences for the university. So-called academic freedom must be abolished, to be replaced by the "Führer principle." (Karl Jaspers reports a private remark by Heidegger at the time that there were too many philosophy professors in Germany, and that two or three would be enough.) The university should no longer be split up into separate faculties and subjects, since all subjects belong to the unified world of the spirit of the German people.

Since the Greeks needed three centuries to firmly pose the question of what knowing really means, the German university cannot expect to achieve this in a few semesters. What is crucial is a willingness to struggle (the German word for struggle is *Kampf*, as in the title of Hitler's book). Teachers and students must join the struggle as comrades, and in this way the new spiritual law of Germany will unfold. But to prepare for this struggle, both teachers and students must become harder, simpler, and less needy in their Dasein than others.

Heidegger closes the lecture by trying to provoke cheers from the crowd: "Do we will the essence of the German university, or don't we?" Answering his own question, he announces that we will our people to fulfill its historic task. The youth of the German nation have already decided this, and they are already on the march in search of their leaders. He ends by finding support in Plato's *Republic*: "everything great stands in the storm." Heidegger's nation would soon face a storm of its own creation.

1933–34: Actions as Rector

The most relevant documents of the rectoral period are contained in a volume of the *Complete Edition* entitled *Reden (Speeches)*. Heidegger later claimed that he accepted the job of rector at the last minute, and only to prevent even worse people from taking power. His friend Professor von Möllendorf had previously been elected as rector, and was supposed to be installed in April 1933. But von Möllendorf was a member of the Social Democratic Party, and this party was already being persecuted by the Nazis, with some of its leading members among the first inmates of the newly established concentration camps. Heidegger and his wife claimed that von Möllendorf begged Heidegger repeatedly to take the job instead. Ultimately, von Möllendorf served for just under a week before he and the University Senate resigned, making way for Heidegger's rise to power. While Heidegger's version of the story may contain some truth, scholars have now established that a group of professors had been scheming for more than a month to install Heidegger in the position, and with the philosopher's full awareness.

That same April, the local Reich Commissioner Robert Wagner had decreed that all Jewish professors should be removed from their posts. It was also Wagner who was responsible for deporting political opponents to concentration camps. On May 9, our philosopher Heidegger sent him a melodramatic telegram professing comradeship and congratulations. Wagner's decree had briefly forced Edmund Husserl from his job. But in the meantime, Wagner's decree was superseded by the nationwide Law on the Reestablishment of a Permanent Civil Service, which made an exception for those "non-Aryan" professors hired before 1918, which included Husserl. By the time the new law was issued, Heidegger was already rector, and so it was Heidegger's job to restore Husserl to his position. In fact, it was Heidegger's wife (a committed Nazi) who did the honors, sending a letter and flowers to Frau Husserl and expressing her regret over "these difficult weeks," in which Edmund Husserl's son Gerhard (a wounded World War I veteran) had also lost his professorship at the University of Kiel. Husserl was appalled despite the flowers, and realized that his friendship with Heidegger was over.

Heidegger was apparently never the crudest sort of biological anti-Semite. Indeed, this would have contradicted his entire philosophy, which leaves no room for such physical concepts as "race." He seems to have made relatively few anti-Semitic statements, even though it would sometimes have been advantageous for him to do so. In an atmosphere soaked with vile racist remarks, Heidegger did not quite sink to the deepest depths.

Nonetheless, we do find a certain cultural anti-Semitism in Heidegger, even in documents predating Hitler's seizure of power. In the struggle for German Dasein, Heidegger does not always seem to think that German citizenship is enough to make one a German. Even after the Rectorate had ended, Heidegger referred to Nietzsche in a speech as "the last great German philosopher." This is a surprising statement. Had he decided that the ethnic Jew Edmund Husserl was not a *great* philosopher, or not a *German* philosopher? One suspects the latter. Rector Heidegger also declared his wish to cleanse the university of "inferior" and "degenerate" elements, which he should have known would have an ominous ring under the circumstances.

On May 4, Heidegger wrote to his brother Fritz. In this letter he encouraged Fritz to join the Party (which never happened), and told him not to think about the dregs of Party membership, but to judge the quality of the movement by the Führer instead. On May 8 we find the first message from Heidegger signed "Sieg Heil!" and on May 22 the first with "Heil Hitler!" Both phrases were repeated frequently over the next year. On May 17, at the university stadium, he followed a broadcast speech by Hitler with these words: "The Chancellor of the Reich, our great Führer, has spoken. The other nations and peoples must now decide . . . To our great Führer Adolf Hitler a German Sieg Heil."

If we were members of Heidegger's legal team in the court of public opinion, there are scattered pieces of evidence we might use to defend him. For instance, the rector did try his best to prevent the firing of the talented Jewish professors Fraenkel and von Hevesy (successfully in the latter case). He also did what he could to find a position abroad for his Jewish assistant, Dr. Werner Brock. Moreover, he seems to have prevented the Nazi students in Freiburg from displaying anti-Semitic posters labeled "Against the Un-German Spirit."

But on the whole, admirable moments are sorely lacking during this period. In response to a letter from Hannah Arendt, Heidegger angrily denied rumors that he was mistreating Jews, though when he lists all the good things he had done for Jews in Freiburg, he manages to make them sound like a major annoyance. During the summer of 1933, Nazis violently stormed a Jewish fraternity building. Heidegger refused to cooperate with the investigation, giving the lame excuse that not all those involved were students. And despite his denials to Arendt, he did begin to distance himself from Jewish friends, students, and colleagues after becoming rector, in some cases explicitly telling friends that "under the circumstances" their contacts would have to cease. Furthermore, he denounced a certain Professor Baumgarten as the friend of a Jew, and also denounced Professor Staudinger (a future Nobel Prize winner) as an ex-pacifist and an opportunist who now falsely claims to be completely in favor of the national awakening. But Heidegger's letter against Baumgarten was dismissed as the product of personal hatred, and the letter against Staudinger was countered by high-level Party support for the famous chemist. As for Husserl, the rumor is untrue that Heidegger banned his former teacher from the university library. But neither did he reach out to ease his great mentor's loneliness. In 1938 he even skipped Husserl's funeral, supposedly because he was sick at home in bed: a grotesque parody of Plato's absence from the death of Socrates. In 1940, Heidegger even removed the famous dedication to Husserl from the reprint of *Being and Time*, although he did retain the complimentary footnote to his teacher.

Many of Heidegger's other troubling statements are widely known. In discussing potential offers to move to the universities of Berlin or Munich, Heidegger stated that he would go wherever he could best serve the work of Adolf Hitler, and wrote tactlessly to his persecuted Jewish friend Elisabeth Blochmann that one of the advantages of Munich would be the chance to "come closer to Hitler." In October of 1933, we hear that "the Führer himself and he alone *is* for today and tomorrow the German reality and its law." On November 25: "I oblige you to the will and the work of our Führer Adolf Hitler." And on January 22, 1934, after complaining that eighteen million Germans belong to the German *Volk* while lying outside the borders of the German Reich (though not for long), he concludes his address with the "threefold Sieg Heil!", his most extravagant version of the salute, and a ludicrous echo of the triple structure of Dasein's temporality.

One is also struck during this period by Heidegger's growing hatred of Christianity, and especially his paranoid fear of Catholic conspiracies. At a somewhat embarrassing Black Forest philosophy camp, dreamed up by Heidegger himself for October 1933, the rector stood by the light of a bonfire and gave speeches denouncing the Christian hatred of life and the world. When a Nazi agreement with the Vatican required a banned Catholic fraternity in Freiburg to be reopened, Heidegger reacted with alarm and even rage over the sinister tactics of the Catholics—for which the German people will someday "pay a price" if they are not careful. Along with the melodramatic October campout, which began with a military-style march of students and young professors from Freiburg to the area near Heidegger's forest hut, Heidegger managed to appear comical in still other ways. At a summer solstice gathering in June, he had pompously addressed the bonfire itself, sounding like a character from a Dungeons and Dragons game.

Most of Heidegger's colleagues detested the strident tone of his university communiqués, and especially resented his enthusiasm for releasing students from class for labor service and military drills. Such resentments had been building from the start, but the tide finally turned against Heidegger when powerful figures in Berlin began to see things the same way. A decision was gradually reached at the top of the government that too many university professors were simply playacting, or engaging in Nazi dress-up games. The decision was reached that these poseurs should finally just shut up and teach, and let the Party officials handle Third Reich ideology. Heidegger came to be seen as one of the more flagrant examples of a useless Nazi playactor.

Although the philosopher later claimed that he resigned as rector to protest the poor treatment of his old Social Democrat friend von Möllendorf, the reality is that his influence within the Nazi movement had waned almost to zero. Heidegger resigned the rectorate almost exactly a year after taking office. Thus ended what was probably the most shameful episode in the history of philosophy. Unfortunately, flashes of the rectoral attitude continued to appear in Heidegger's writings from time to time in later years. But for the most part, he entered a kind of internal exile within the Reich, increasingly embittered by his surroundings.

7

Hermit in the Reich

His paws bloodied by the failure of the rectorate, Heidegger returned to a more private existence. There is no question that he remained sympathetic to the Nazi movement well beyond 1934, as is clear from various eyewitness reports and from disturbing remarks in his own writings (there are at least two explicit toasts to Hitler and Mussolini in lecture courses of the period). Even so, Heidegger was clearly disappointed by his inability to shape university reform in the Third Reich, and seems to have given up such ambitions permanently. The usual interpretation of this period is that Heidegger licked his wounds by withdrawing into the past intellectual glories of Germany and ancient Greece. This view strikes me as basically correct.

The dominant figures for Heidegger during this period were the philosopher Friedrich Nietzsche and the poet Friedrich Hölderlin, both the subject of multiple manuscripts during these years. There is also the cryptic book-length work *Contributions to Philosophy*, a strange production that remains fascinating even if traditional Heideggerians overestimate its importance. My own view is that Heidegger experienced a brief intellectual resurgence in 1935, since this was the year of two of his best works of the decade: the widely popular lecture course *Introduction to Metaphysics* and the influential essay "On the Origin of the Work of Art." During this period, the seeds were planted for Heidegger's intellectual rebirth after the war.

1935: Inner Truth and Greatness

In the summer semester of 1935, Heidegger gave a lecture course entitled *Introduction to Metaphysics,* published as a book two decades later in slightly altered form. It has long been one of the philosopher's best-selling paperbacks in English-speaking countries, and is the first book by Heidegger that many readers encounter.

WHY SOMETHING AND NOT NOTHING?

"Why are there beings rather than nothing?" This is the opening question of the semester. Heidegger is not looking for an answer from either religion or physics. Indeed, he is not looking for an answer at all, but is simply trying to jolt us from our absorption in the everyday presence of beings. Wondering about this question is part of being human. "Why are there beings rather than nothing?" Each of us is touched by this question from time to time, though usually we suppress it. Only a handful of humans asks it explicitly. The question comes upon us in fundamental moods: in moments of profound despair, rejoicing, or boredom, the world seems to detach itself from us, and we wonder that it exists at all.

It is the widest question, since it relates to everything that is; it is the deepest question, since it touches the utmost depths of the world; it is the most fundamental question, because it does not speak about any particular kind of being, but covers them all. Although Heidegger is usually obsessed with human Dasein, he concedes in this course that the basic questions of philosophy pertain to an elephant in an Indian jungle or a chemical combustion process on Mars no less than to Dasein. In fact, he states that humans are ultimately rather unimportant beings: swarming, bewildered animals who imagine that they have discovered knowledge.

Heidegger is not bothered that few people take the question of being seriously. Philosophy is always ahead of its time, and becomes popular in its own time only if it is superficial or completely misunderstood. Although philosophy has no practical use, it can still be a force in the world. In perhaps the most brilliant answer ever given to the question "what can you do with philosophy?" Heidegger replies: we do not do anything with philosophy, *it does something with us.* Philosophy makes things harder rather than easier, but in this way it opens up paths to be followed by the destiny of nations.

NATURE AND *PHYSIS*

Heidegger now turns to the word "metaphysics" itself, without giving a complete history of it. He is actually more interested in the "physics" part of the term. The Greek word *physis* means "nature," and hence physics is the study of nature. But the English/German word "nature/*Natur*" comes from a Latin root, *natura*, and Heidegger is no admirer of the Latin language. He sees the translation of Greek philosophical terms into Latin as a grievous process through which the Greek experience of the world is trivialized, giving a hollow and self-evident ring to the mysteries of ancient Greek Dasein. For Heidegger, *physis* is not simply "nature," but the sprouting and emerging of being from concealment. Only philosophy, not physics, can do justice to *physis*. Philosophy is one of the few truly great human achievements, and what is great must always have great beginnings and great endings.

Although the title of his lecture course refers to metaphysics, this is almost always a negative term for Heidegger. Metaphysics is the type of philosophy, dominant from Plato through Nietzsche, which answers the question of being with the name of one particular highest being that explains or dominates the others. Metaphysics is unable to approach being itself, and fundamental moods such as despair or rejoicing take us beyond all metaphysics by putting us in direct contact with the question of being. The mood of Angst puts us in direct contact with nothingness, and nothingness goes hand in hand with being, for being is finite and only becomes accessible against the empty background of the "not." While metaphysics and science remain trapped on the surface-world of presence, there are ways to move beyond this surface. Along with fundamental moods, great poetry takes us to a new place as well. Poetry is greater than science because poetry hints into the depths, and as we have seen already, hinting is the only way to approach those depths.

THINGS

Foreshadowing his later essay "The Thing," Heidegger continues in his newfound appreciation that human Dasein is not the only topic of philosophy. There are countless beings, all of them equally real: crowds, trees, rivers, the Japanese, Bach's fugues, and criminals. More specifically, consider a piece of chalk. The chalk can be used for writing, and this is a quality that belongs to *the chalk itself*, and is not simply projected onto the chalk by us. If the chalk had no features of its own, we would never need to pick up the chalk specifically when writing, but could just as easily project writing ability onto other objects such as stones or trees.

To give another example, consider a building such as a high school. Heidegger observes that the building is there whether we look at it or not. We do not recognize it as a high school by making a list of properties viewed by our senses and then imagine that all these properties must somehow be unified in a bundle. Instead, we encounter the school as a unified thing from the start. It has the look and feel of a high school about it: or as Heidegger puts it, "the smell" of a high school.

TECHNOLOGY AND THE GERMANS

This sense for the deeper reality of things has been ruined by technology, which reduces things to objects—mere surfaces of useful qualities produced and manipulated by industry. For Heidegger, this dismal technological hysteria is embodied to an equal degree by the United States and by Soviet Communism. Hitler's Germany in 1935 is squeezed between the Americans and the Soviets as if between two great pincers. Germany is the most endangered nation, surrounded by more neighbors than anyone else. Yet Germany is also the most *metaphysical* nation—presumably in the good sense of the term, just as America and Russia are the most metaphysical nations in the bad sense of reducing things to sheer presence. The world is darkening. The gods have fled, the earth is being laid waste, all humans are becoming interchangeable and standardized, and mediocrity has begun to dominate. The human spirit has degenerated into superficial intelligence and cleverness, and no one speaks with a sense of danger anymore. Even language has become infested with corny and trivial slang, and a nation's language is a sign of its relation to being.

Yet Germany may still be able to save Europe. Civilization in Europe can only be saved by new spiritual energies unfolding from its center, in a new relation to being. Heidegger still seems confident that the Nazi regime has a role to play in this relation to being. Although he does attack the superficial philosophy of Nazi propagandists, this is only because they have nothing to do with "the inner truth and greatness" of the movement.

MISUNDERSTANDINGS OF BEING

He closes the semester with a lengthy analysis of four classical misunderstandings of being, which we can summarize briefly here. Traditionally, being is distinguished from becoming, from appearance, from thinking, and from the "ought." When being is contrasted with becoming, it is supposed to be that which endures without change. When being is distinguished from appearance, it is seen as that which is truly real behind the veil of illusion, fully and permanently present. When being is defined as the opposite of thinking, it is seen as a constant unyielding target that thought attempts to approach. And when being is contrasted with what ought to be, it is viewed as something stubbornly present that ought to be surpassed. In all four cases, being is defined as *enduring presence*. According to Heidegger, every episode in the history of philosophy has followed at least one of these paths, but all four lead to the same error of conceiving of being as presence.

As a remedy to this ancient dogma, Heidegger suggests that we view being instead as *temporality*. Our own miserable epoch of being as enduring presence, which has broadened into the dismal wasteland of American and Soviet technology, can be counteracted only by considering the temporality of being. But the new epoch cannot be purposely triggered by the books of Martin Heidegger, he says. What we really must do is wait. Questioning means waiting, even if one has to wait for a lifetime.

1935: Earth and World in the Artwork

In November of 1935, Heidegger lectured in Freiburg on "The Origin of the Work of Art," repeating the lecture in Zürich the following year. This is one of Heidegger's most beloved writings, and certainly one of his most charming. The "origin" of the work of art does not mean its historical beginning in the Stone Age, but something more like "essence." The origin of the artwork is that which makes it what it truly is. Heidegger's lecture tries to define the essence of art, which turns out to be strife between earth and world.

MATTER AND FORM

The usual understanding of works of art, as of most objects, is that they are composed of matter and form. A statue is marble shaped into the form of a hero, or jewelry is gold in the form of a necklace. According to Heidegger, the belief that things are made of form and matter is a result of their being regarded as useful tools, since hammers and chisels are matter shaped into a specific form. But what we are looking for in our discussion of art is the reality of things, quite apart from their usefulness or the fact that they were produced; we are trying to grasp things in their own essence, not in their relation to handy human purposes.

On this note, Heidegger returns to the structure of equipment, as a negative example to show what we are trying to avoid when thinking about artworks. He asks us to consider a pair of peasant shoes. These shoes are produced with a specific purpose in mind: maybe fieldwork or dancing. In each of these cases, the matter and form of the shoes will be different—work shoes need to be made of sturdier material and generally have a less ornate appearance than those used for dancing festivals. The usefulness of these shoes comes from their reliability; the better the shoes are, the less we notice them. But over time, the shoes become worn out, and their reliability gradually erodes.

For Heidegger, such concepts are irrelevant when discussing artworks: pieces of art are *works*, not just tools or present-at-hand physical lumps. The essence of art is that it shows the truth of beings set to work. What artworks reproduce is not things, but rather the *essence* of things. Normally, equipment is used invisibly and silently until it breaks down or otherwise attracts our notice. Only in artworks does the equipmentality of equipment come to the fore. While tools tend to be invisibly immersed in the world, in the artwork the tool's entire world becomes visible along with it. It so happens that the tool's world comes into open strife with *earth*. Earth is the unseen, inexhaustible depth of things. In Van Gogh's famous painting of the peasant shoes (Heidegger is wrong: they were actually Van Gogh's own shoes), the shoes are no longer reliable tools, and neither are they simple pieces of leather and string. The shoes incarnate the strife of world and earth, thereby revealing the essence of the shoes.

Gaining proper access to an artwork is difficult, since this requires that we view the work in isolation from its everyday relations. Heidegger says that this possibility is especially ruined by the art industry, which reduces artworks to objects sold and transported like coal. It is also ruined by the cult of personality that surrounds artists in our time, since in great art that the artist should become an unimportant passageway toward the work. But to view a work in isolation does not mean to see it in a bare white room in a museum or gallery. An artwork belongs in the very space that it opens up for us. Heidegger chooses a Greek temple as his example, since it does not represent any other object, as paintings and sculptures usually do. Standing on a rock against the storm, the temple is what first makes the rock and storm visible as what they are. It also lets numerous other surrounding objects be visible as what they are: tree, grass, eagle, bull, snake, and cricket.

This emergence into visibility is what the Greeks called *physis*. The ground on which all of these things stand is the sheltering earth. The temple brings these things from the earth and sets them up in a world. The world worlds, as Heidegger strangely puts it, and this worlding of the world creates a space in which the protection and grace of the gods is either granted or withheld. A stone has no world. Plants and animals also have no world, but are only bound to their surroundings. By contrast, a peasant woman does have a world, because she dwells amidst the openness of beings. With this example, Heidegger makes a value judgment that not only ranks humans above animals and plants, but also ranks peasant women above urban industrialists and stockbrokers. Apparently, even if all human Dasein has a world, this is even more true of some Daseins than others. Heidegger's preference for the rural over the urban is clearly visible in his writings and in his own life.

The strife of earth and world is best seen in artworks, not tools. After all, tools are designed in such a way that the material vanishes, enabling the tool to function easily. If we are constantly focused on the metal or plastic in our cars, this is probably because these materials are somehow inefficient or uncomfortable. In artworks, by contrast, it is better for the material *not* to vanish, since only in this way can the strife between earth and world occur. Only in artworks do rock, metal, and color first become what they are rather than being absorbed and suppressed by some ulterior function. Both masons and sculptors use stone. The difference is that the mason *uses up* the stone by fully assigning it to some practical purpose, while the sculptor lets the stone shine forth as what it is. In a sculpture the earth comes forth, yet it remains a shelter. By showing the earth *as* a shelter rather than as material useful for our purposes, it is what first lets the earth be earth.

Earth is self-secluding, always hiding from view. For this reason, the artist is able to bring earth forth only "as" self-secluding. Earth strikes down any attempt to penetrate or objectify it; earth remains a hidden shelter, always in strife with world. There is an endless interplay of the two terms—world is grounded on earth, and earth juts through world. World and earth are belligerent by nature, endlessly in strife. Beauty is the shining of earth as earth, made visible in world.

We now turn from the work itself to the process of artistic creation. Since the truth of the artwork is a duel between clearing and concealing, it needs to be *founded*. Truth is the strife of clearing and concealing (that is to say, of world and earth). The strife between these two terms is not an unbridgeable rift, but more like a deep intimacy in which the two terms belong together, reflected in one another. This never happens in tool-making, in which the tool is finished as soon as it has been properly fashioned. There is no ongoing strife between the material of a tool and its function, unless it is an unusually bad tool, or an exceptionally beautiful one that reaches the level of art. Art is essentially a thrusting movement into the realm of the awe-inspiring. As soon as art is reduced to a familiar set of images prized by connoisseurs, we have entered the art business—which for Heidegger is not a good thing. The thrust of art into the realm of the awe-inspiring is also a thrust into a people's history, transmitting the people into its appointed historic task: not harmless words in the Germany of 1935. Although Heidegger's examples in this essay largely concern visual art, he closes the essay by saying that all art is essentially *poetry*. Already, he was in the midst of a fateful dialogue with his favorite poet—Friedrich Hölderlin.

1936: The Echo of Hölderlin

Heidegger's first lectures on Hölderlin came in 1934–35, just before the essay on artworks. He continued to cover Hölderlin intermittently in his lecture courses until 1942. His famous courses on the poet deal with the hymns entitled *Germanien, Der Rhein, Der Ister*, and *Andenken*. There is also a collection of shorter essays with the title *Elucidations of Hölderlin's Poetry*, now available in English. Given the difficulties of discussing the longer courses, I will focus here on "Hölderlin and the Essence of Poetry," a short lecture delivered in 1936 in Rome (where, incidentally, Heidegger's former student Karl Löwith encountered him still wearing a swastika pin in his lapel.) Since some readers may be unfamiliar with Hölderlin, a brief biographical sketch is in order.

THE LIFE OF HÖLDERLIN

Friedrich Hölderlin is one of Germany's most celebrated poets, and his early lapse into insanity makes him perhaps the most tragic as well. He was born in 1770 in the village of Lauffen in Swabia, not far from Stuttgart. Early in life, he lost his father and then his stepfather. His pious mother hoped that Friedrich would someday enter the clergy, and with this in mind, the eighteen-year-old entered the famous seminary in Tübingen. There, he befriended the future philosophers Hegel and Schelling, forming the most impressive trio of schoolboy friends the world has ever known; many scholars think the future poet actually had an important *philosophical* influence on his friends. The student Hölderlin was remembered as an elegant, handsome, and somewhat otherworldly youth with a deep love for the Greek classics.

Following graduation he found that he had no interest in pursuing a religious career. He drifted around Germany a bit, attended the key lectures of philosopher J. G. Fichte in Jena, and befriended the older poet Friedrich Schiller. It was Schiller who found Hölderlin his first position as a house tutor to wealthy families. Jobs of this kind often involved humiliating treatment from arrogant and ill-mannered employers. Especially destabilizing for Hölderlin was his tutoring work in Frankfurt for the Gontard family, as Hölderlin fell deeply in love with the young wife of the household, Suzette Gontard (called "Diotima" by Hölderlin, after the wise character who advised Socrates about love). Diotima seems to have fallen in love with Hölderlin as well, though the relationship may have remained chaste. After nearly three years with the family, Hölderlin lost his position. Already showing signs of mental disturbance, he failed in his efforts to become a lecturer in Greek in Jena, and was forced to accept another tutoring position in Bordeaux, France, arriving there on foot. In 1802, Suzette Gontard died, and Hölderlin left Bordeaux for his mother's home, arriving in an advanced state of mental breakdown from which he had only a brief and partial recovery.

He spent the last thirty-six years of his life in a state of complete insanity, living in a tower along the peaceful river Neckar in Tübingen, the same town where he had attended seminary. He died in the early summer of 1843, at the age of seventy-three, mourned by almost no one. Although Hölderlin's poems were admired by such great figures as Nietzsche and Dilthey, it was not until the early twentieth century that Hölderlin reached his present degree of fame. The young Heidegger was so deeply affected by his encounter with Hölderlin's poems that it is not possible to overstate his admiration for the poet. For Heidegger, Hölderlin is not just a poetic craftsman, but one of the central figures in German history, and even in the future of the human race as a whole.

Hölderlin's poems tend to be dense with imagery, and are usually written in Greek-inspired hexameter (six stresses per line), unlike the pentameter (five stresses per line) which is far more common in English and German poetry. Here I will attempt a brief sample, with the first stanza of the hymn *Homecoming*:

Deep in the Alps, the night is shining bright. And the cloud,
joyfully forming, covers over the gaping vale.
Turbulent, laughing mountain air, this way and that;
suddenly, down through the pine trees shines and dwindles a ray.

Joyful, shivering chaos slowly hurries to battle.
Young in form, but strong, it revels in loving strife.
Brewing, wavering under the rocks in timeless barriers,
morning rises in Bacchic frenzy, deep inside.

There the year grows endlessly. Holy hours and days,
ordered more boldly than ever, mix together some way.
Even so, the storm bird marks the time amidst mountains;
high in the air he tarries, waiting to summon the day.

Deep below, the little village also awakens.
Fearless, under the peaks, gazing as always on high.
Sensing growth, with ancient springs streaming like lightning;
under the crashing waters, steam and moisture rise.

Echoes resound. The workplace stretches far beyond measure,
stirring its arms, sending gifts by day and night.

THE POET OF POETRY

In the essay "Hölderlin and the Essence of Poetry," Heidegger
begins with a question and a confession. Why focus on Hölderlin?
After all, Homer, Sophocles, Virgil, Dante, Shakespeare, and
Goethe all seem to realize the essence of poetry even more richly
than Hölderlin, whom few critics would place in the same rank as
these six giants of world literature. (It is interesting that Heidegger
has little to say in his career about any of these other figures, with
the exception of a few passages on Sophocles.) The reason we
focus on Hölderlin is because he is the poet who writes about
poetry. He is the poet's poet, or the poet of poetry itself. In what
sense does Hölderlin write poetry about poetry? In this simple
essay, Heidegger gives us five brief pointers on Hölderlin.

FIVE POINTERS ON HÖLDERLIN

The first two pointers seem to contradict one another. Pointer
number one is found in a letter to his mother in 1799, where
Hölderlin calls poetry the most innocent of occupations. But in a
letter written the very next year, he says (and this is pointer number
two) that poetry is the most dangerous of possessions. Since poetry
arises in language, we can rephrase our questions as follows: who
possesses language, and in what sense is it dangerous? Heidegger
answers that language belongs to Dasein, and the essence of language is *intimacy*, which brings things together even while keeping
them apart. The danger of language is that it poses a threat to being
itself, through the allure of individual beings, which hypnotize us
with their surface presence and cause us to forget their underlying
ground. The danger of language stems from its ambiguity, which
can make the inessential look essential, while also making the essential seem shallow. Language is not just a tool for pointing at the
world, but rather is the only thing that allows Dasein to stand in the

openness of beings, with all the dangers this entails. Heidegger often cites Hölderlin's lines that danger and saving power always go together. Poetry is both danger and saving power (the same will later turn out to be true of technology). In the face of this danger, Hölderlin eventually collapsed into madness. In Heidegger's view, this was not a biographical accident that could have been prevented with therapy or psychiatric drugs. Madness was Hölderlin's fate, since "the first fruits always belong to the gods," and Hölderlin was the most tragic of first fruits in German history.

The third pointer about Hölderlin is as follows: humankind only exists in language, and language is always a conversation. A conversation involves both speaking and hearing, and neither is possible unless being and beings shine forth to us. This can only happen for humans, because only Dasein is *temporal*—only Dasein finds itself in the midpoint where beings emerge from unconcealment in some specific way. Language is what names the gods, even though the gods remain hidden from us and only hint at what they are. Heidegger is not referring here to a specific set of gods (particular deities from various world religions) but is simply invoking the plurality of what remains hidden from us. Language is the place where we negotiate whether and how we yield to the gods or withhold ourselves from them by remaining tossed about on the surface of the presence of beings.

The fourth pointer comes from one of Hölderlin's own lines of poetry: "but what endures is founded by poets." Even that which is permanent and enduring in the world needs to be set down or established, or else it will remain mixed in with the tumult and confusion of the world and never take on clear form. Beings as a whole become manifest to us; for this to happen, Dasein must stand in an open space. Yet Dasein does not just see things sitting around independently and give names to each of them. Instead, the poet first names each thing as what it is, and only this naming establishes the things. Being itself, and the essence of specific beings, are never visible at a glance as soon as we open our eyes, but must first be created and founded. This gives poets a central role in human existence.

The fifth and final pointer comes from another famous poetic saying of Hölderlin: "poetically man dwells on this earth." To dwell poetically on the earth means to stand amidst the presence of the hidden but hinting gods, which brings us into closer proximity to the essence of things. Existence is founded or established by poets, yet is still a gift given to us beyond all our powers of decision. Even so, poetry is not just a game that plays with pre-established words and grammatical rules. Poetry shapes the essence of language, and thereby shapes the relation of a people to its historic destiny. The poet intercepts signs from the gods and passes them along to his or her people. The poet has been cast into a space between humans and gods, and this is obviously not just a game—as Hölderlin's madness proves. Another famous line of Hölderlin speaks of Oedipus, who put out his own eyes: "perhaps King Oedipus has an eye too many." As Heidegger says, perhaps Friedrich Hölderlin has an eye too many. He is the poet of our time of distress, in which the old gods have fled and the new ones have not yet arrived. Hölderlin's madness resulted from his keeping a lonely watch for his people, creating truth for them, even as no one cared.

1936–38: The Other Beginning

From 1936–38, Heidegger worked privately on an odd, lengthy manuscript entitled *Contributions to Philosophy*, which was not published until his centennial year of 1989. It had long been rumored as Heidegger's second great masterwork, and was immediately toasted as a work of genius when it finally appeared. Due in part to the great obscurity of this book, some of the initial enthusiasm has died down. Even so, *Contributions* remains one of Heidegger's most hypnotic productions, and cannot be left out of any survey of his philosophy.

The subtitle of the book is *Vom Ereignis*, which the recently published English translation renders as *From Enowning*—a needlessly bizarre choice, in my view. A simpler and more literal translation of the subtitle would be *On the Event*. We have already seen that "event" is a major word for Heidegger even in the earliest portion of his career, and there is no good reason to assume that it means anything radically different in the 1930s from what it did in 1919. Recall that even for the younger Heidegger, things are not present-at-hand products or ideas, but events that partially withdraw from all attempts to grasp them. *Contributions to Philosophy* is simply the next of Heidegger's many attempts to describe the event of being.

HEIDEGGER'S NUMEROLOGY

Although *Contributions* seems painfully obscure on a first reading, it has the same deep simplicity as all his works. Too little attention has been paid to the shifting numerology of Heidegger's philosophy. His basic concepts always come in groups of two, three, four, five, or six. Since Heidegger is the least empirical of thinkers, we know that he is not coming up with these numbers by looking at philosophical problems on a case-by-case basis. The twofold structures always refer to the endless interplay in his thinking between absence and presence, veiling and unveiling, sheltering and clearing, or being and beings. This twofold is Heidegger's most powerful central idea, one that allows him to challenge all forms of presence and thereby claim to be starting philosophy from a new beginning.

The threefolds are equally easy, since they always refer back to the structure of temporality, no matter how ingenious Heidegger is at coining endless new names for the same recurring trio of terms. Dasein is thrown into a world (past), yet also projects possibilities upon this world (future), with these two terms always meeting in a unified center (the present, in Heidegger's new ambiguous sense). The fourfold and fivefold will be discussed later in this book. *Contributions to Philosophy* is the shining hour of a sixfold structure.

Heidegger openly states that his book will discuss six key terms, all of them belonging together in the "jointure" of a unified onefold. These six terms of the *Contributions* amount to a simple doubling of the structure of temporality, through a mutual interplay between the threefold first beginning of philosophy and another threefold beginning. For Heidegger, this other beginning is not just the lucky result of his own individual efforts, but is the only *possible* other beginning of philosophy. The first beginning was dominated by being in the form of presence, while the other beginning starts from Heidegger's alternative of being as hiding and sending itself in various epochs. Although he mostly recommends calmness, patient waiting, and listening into the distance rather than trying too hard to start the new era, he clearly thinks that we live in a very special time in history. Our age is heroic despite its grim desolation. Being itself has begun to resound amidst the nightmarish wasteland of planetary technology.

Contributions contains 281 sections, ranging in length from a few sentences to more than ten pages. In one sense, it feels like a highly disorganized work: in most cases the sections could be shuffled and redealt in random order without either lessening or improving the reader's understanding. But in another sense, the book is tightly organized around its six key terms. The current English translation gives these as follows: *echo, playing-forth, leap, grounding, the ones to come,* and *the last god.* As wild as these terms may sound, they arise from a simple process. Three of them reflect the temporal structure of the first, Greek beginning of philosophy; the other three stem from the temporal structure of the new beginning of philosophy, the only possible new beginning. Echo, the leap, and the ones to come belong to our new beginning, while playing-forth, grounding, and the last god arise from the interplay with the Greek beginning. Before discussing in greater detail how these terms function for Heidegger, we should say a few words about the lengthy preface to the book.

THE PREFACE TO *CONTRIBUTIONS*

The title *Contributions to Philosophy* already has a tone of cutting sarcasm about it. Heidegger always had limitless contempt for mainstream academic philosophy, and he relishes the mocking use of a dull academic title that seems to belong on a musty library shelf. The acid tones of the book continue throughout, as when Heidegger refers to "the people of today, who are scarcely worth mentioning as one turns away from them." Such haughty dismissiveness, which is also found in many of the writings of Nietzsche, seems to hark back to the pre-Socratic era of philosophy, with its lordly thinkers denouncing the masses and leaping to their deaths in volcanic craters. Somewhat to Heidegger's credit, the book is also lightly sprinkled with nasty remarks about official Nazi racial ideology, and even contains one mild dig at anti-Semitism.

The really essential title of the book, he says, is the subtitle *Vom Ereignis: On the Event.* The event of being is the truth of being, in which being manifests itself in some specific way even while remaining sheltered. Heidegger even tells us that this is his one and only thought, and I see no reason to disagree. The theme of the truth of being was never grasped by the first beginning in Greece, which unconsciously followed the guiding question: what is a being? The other beginning of philosophy, the only other pos-sible beginning, follows the fundamental question: what is the truth of being? The time of philosophical systems is over, and the time for rebuilding the essential shape of beings from out of the truth of being has not yet arrived. We are stranded in an interme-diate time marked by great distress. But only this distress will give us enough force to escape metaphysics and its dismal parade of presence-at-hand.

One key to making such an escape is the strife between hidden earth and visible world that was mentioned in the artwork essay. Another key is the newly defined sixfold "jointure" of thinking, which is unified in a simple onefold. Each of the six terms names the same onefold. Heidegger makes it easy for us to arrange the six, since he begins with four of the terms, leaving the other two as their unifying center. Echo and playing-forth belong to what Heidegger calls "soil," thereby relating them to the earth that hides and shelters itself (past). By contrast, the leap and the grounding are defined as openness, thereby relating them to world (future). Finally, those who are to come and the last god belong at the center of this structure, unifying it (present).

Echo resounds from the distress of the abandonment of being by beings. Our age of nihilism only values progress, and such progress merely produces a greater number of increasingly gigan-tic and shallow objects. We have entered the age of calculation, acceleration, and vulgarity. All entities are entirely used up and mobilized to serve various purposes, and all sense of the ambigu-ous depth of things is lost. Philosophy will soon be expelled from a university system dominated by cybernetics and journalism. Nonetheless, by exposing us to this deep distress, echo also launches the other beginning of philosophy. Being is mistreated and forgotten, yet being resounds through the madness of our age precisely at the moment when it has been most suppressed.

The term *playing-forth* should be thought of as a playing *back and forth*, as when two soccer players pass the ball to one another. If echo is the scream of forgotten being from amidst the reign of technology, the playing-forth involves the relation between the two beginnings of philosophy. Playing-forth is historical in its very essence. These two terms, then, refer to the being that is concealed or already given to us (past). While echo is being's call of distress into the present, the playing-forth is the tension or interplay

The Sixfold, Comprising a Onefold

association	sixfold term	temporal position (in threefold)
world	**leap**: a daring leap into the event of being, a leap that expects nothing	future
	grounding: the leap must be grounded in the sheltering darkness of history	
unifying center	**those who are to come**: like-minded strangers who face the ambiguous status of being as both giving and concealing, and are alert to the truth of being as the basic principle of the other beginning	present
	the last god: remains hidden; it is the last one because the other beginning will not need to keep finding new gods	
soil	**echo**: the abandonment of being in the distracting dominance of beings	past
	playing forth: the tension between the first beginning ("what are beings?") and the only other possible beginning ("what is the truth of being itself?")	

between the first beginning ("what are beings?") and the only other possible beginning ("what is the truth of being itself?").

By contrast, *leap* and *grounding* are futural terms. Heidegger defines the leap as a daring jump that expects nothing: a bold vault into the new beginning. The broadest leap of all is thinking, which moves us into a new open space. Whenever Heidegger speaks about the future, he almost always speaks about death, and the same happens here. The enactment of being-towards-death, he says, is a duty for the thinkers of the other beginning. The leap is a leap into the event of being, which opens up a crevice in the world—a strife between world and earth.

Just as playing-forth drew echo down into the historic depths of the first beginning, *grounding* does the same thing for the leap. Dasein itself is the crossing between the first and other beginnings of philosophy. While the leap is a gesture of pure daring, it also draws its force from the deepest history of human being. Only the steadfastness of Dasein lets the ground be ground. Grounding forces the leap to be grounded in the sheltering darkness of history.

This leaves us with *the ones to come* and *the last god*, which are stationed at the center of the other four terms. Heidegger speaks in surprisingly concrete fashion of the ones to come: he estimates that a small number of such people are already alive and in our midst, unrecognized. They are like-minded strangers who resolutely face the ambiguity of being as both giving and concealing, and are thereby alert to the truth of being as the basic principle of the other beginning. Hölderlin is their patron poet, since he looks ahead further than anyone else. But these futural ones are also approached by the hint of the last god, who remains hidden.

The *last god* is not an actual deity, but a new highest principle for guiding human action. Although a religious spirit pervades the whole of Heidegger's career, it is a largely pagan spirit rather than a Catholic one, despite his Jesuit seminary background. This god is the last one because the other beginning will not need to continue dipping endlessly into the pool of history for new gods. By receiving the hint of the last god, we renew the world by rescuing the earth from oblivion. This god needs humans to be the founders of the strife of earth and world.

There are numerous additional themes in *Contributions* that we cannot discuss here, such as space-time, the abyss, and a host of colorful new fundamental moods. The preceding focus on the six key terms of the book should provide a good rough orientation for any reader who wishes to delve more deeply into this cryptic work. However, there are many other books by Heidegger that one ought to read before this one. The continuing claims that *Contributions* is Heidegger's second major work are greatly exaggerated.

1940: The Metaphysics of Nietzsche

Heidegger's best-known works on Nietzsche are the lecture courses that began in 1936–37 and were eventually reworked into the widely read volumes known simply as *Nietzsche*. Since a discussion of that massive work would take more space than the present book can spare, I will focus instead on a clearer and shorter volume entitled "Nietzsche's Metaphysics." This brief treatise of less than a hundred pages was written in 1940, and is not yet available in English. It was supposed to provide the basis for a lecture course the following year, but was replaced at the last minute by yet another course on Hölderlin. "Nietzsche's Metaphysics" goes far beyond any treatment of Nietzsche, and points us directly toward Heidegger's own philosophical path after World War II.

Nietzsche, like Hölderlin, is a great intellectual figure of nineteenth-century Germany who eventually lost his sanity. Here as in Hölderlin's case, Heidegger would never accept that Nietzsche's insanity was caused by physical maladies such as syphilis, a brain tumor, or a chemical imbalance, as most theories of his madness hold. Instead, Nietzsche resembled Hölderlin in bearing a terrible burden of solitude, making him another of those "first fruits" harvested by the gods. Although Heidegger in his loneliness seems to identify with both of these figures, their differences in temperament are striking. Despite his psychological problems after World War II, and despite certain Nazi attacks on his philosophy as "schizophrenic," it is hard to imagine a more stable temperament than Heidegger's, or to imagine a philosopher less likely to have gone insane himself. The image of Martin Heidegger collapsing in a public square and spending a decade in a state of madness approaches the point of comedy.

THE LIFE OF NIETZSCHE

Friedrich Nietzsche was born in 1844 in the tiny village of Röcken near Leipzig, a small-town boy just like Hölderlin and Heidegger. Nietzsche lost his father at a young age and moved with his family to nearby Naumburg. This appealing town is home to the famous classical boarding school known as Schulpforta, where Nietzsche later obtained a scholarship. Following graduation from the school, with outstanding marks for his work in Greek and Latin, he attended the Universities of Bonn and Leipzig, where he studied classical philology. While in Leipzig he met the composer Richard Wagner at the home of an acquaintance. After receiving a professorship in Basel, Switzerland, at the age of twenty-five, he lived very close to the Swiss estate of the Wagners, and soon became close friends with both Richard and his wife Cosima. His first book, *The Birth of Tragedy*, praised Wagner for the supposed revival of Greek tragedy in his operas. His later works took an increasing distance from Wagner and his circle, finally leading to a complete break between the friends.

In 1879, at age thirty-five, Nietzsche retired from the University of Basel due to chronic health problems, and spent the rest of his life traveling between Switzerland, Italy, and southern France. A disastrous end to his friendship with the young author Lou von Salomé spurred him to write *Thus Spoke Zarathustra*, his most poetic work. Throughout the 1880s, Nietzsche wrote books of increasing intensity, darkened by gathering clouds of megalomania. In early 1889, he collapsed in a public square in Turin, Italy, after witnessing the beating of a horse. He never recovered his sanity, and spent most of the remaining eleven years of his life under the care of his sister Elisabeth, an anti-Semite and eventual Nazi best known for falsifying many of her brother's manuscripts. At the time of his death in 1900, he was already becoming widely known, but his great burst of mass popularity came at about the same time as Hölderlin's— around the period of World War I. Nietzsche is perhaps most famous as a formidable critic of religion, and is generally regarded as the most brilliant literary stylist in philosophy since Plato.

THE FIVEFOLD STRUCTURE OF NIETZSCHE'S PHILOSOPHY

We now turn to "Nietzsche's Metaphysics," written by Heidegger in 1940. This brief work has been completely overshadowed by his celebrated multivolume book *Nietzsche*. But as Heidegger says in a footnote to the 1940 treatise, Nietzsche's metaphysics is actually much easier to understand than he had been able to show in the larger work. It is hard to disagree with this assessment. Indeed, there are few writings by Heidegger on *any* subject that are as systematically organized as this short draft on Nietzsche. While the *Contributions to Philosophy* described a sixfold jointure of the world, "Nietzsche's Metaphysics" shifts gears by offering a *fivefold* world. As will be seen shortly, this fivefold is simply a fourfold held together by a unifying central term.

As Heidegger sees it, Nietzsche is a metaphysician, just like all philosophers since Plato. In this context the word "metaphysics" is meant in the bad sense: namely, Nietzsche is unaware of the truth and concealment of being, and merely seeks one highest being that explains all the rest. Instead of picking out one key term in all of Nietzsche's writings, Heidegger identifies *five*.

The *eternal return* is Nietzsche's doctrine that all events, no matter how trivial, will repeat themselves an infinite number of times in the future; even our most miserable and tedious moments will be relived again and again. The *will to power* is his notion that all living and nonliving things have their own perspective on the universe, and seek to unleash their force and impose their own perspective on other entities. The *superman* is the human who is strong enough to embrace the theory of eternal return and thereby rise beyond the mediocre humanity of the modern "last man," who cares only for comfort and bland happiness. *Nihilism* is the situation of modern Europe, in which God has died and all values have lost their meaning.

For Heidegger, these four terms are unified in a lesser-known fifth term that is mentioned only occasionally in Nietzsche's writings: *Gerechtigkeit*, which we can simply call *justice*. By arranging these key terms in a pattern, Heidegger approaches the breakthrough of his own "fourfold," the mysterious concept announced after the war in Bremen. (See the next chapter.) The eternal return, will to power, superman, and nihilism are engaged in a relation of *strife*, says Heidegger, continuing the theme that emerged from the artwork essay. All four terms are both near and distant with respect to one another. Their unification by *justice* show a striking link between Heidegger and the ancient Greek philosopher Anaximander of Miletus. For Anaximander, the existence of opposites in the world is a form of injustice, and each term (hot, cold, spicy, living, white) must pay a penalty by eventually passing away along with its opposite. By contrast, Heidegger's own concept of justice holds its four constituent terms in a kind of permanent strife or instability. Justice will not be attained at some point millions of years in the future, as seems to be Anaximander's view.

This is the first version of the fourfold in Heidegger's philosophy: the result of two intercrossing axes of division. Heidegger had already been speaking for a number of years about the difference between beings as such (essence) and as a whole (existence). For

Nietzsche, the essence of beings as such is *will to power*, since he defines beings as perspectives, and as the force of mastery by which one being exerts its own perspective on the others. The way that beings are as a whole is *eternal return*, since each entity that exists happens only amidst an endless recurrence that encompasses them all.

If will to power and eternal return refer to how beings really are, Heidegger says that the other two terms refer to the "history" of beings as such and as a whole: in other words, they refer to the "truth" or "visibility" of beings as such and as a whole. The parallel term to the eternal return is the *superman*, who is strong enough to bear this most horrifying of thoughts and thus become liberated from the spirit of revenge against what is past. The term corresponding to the will to power is *nihilism*, in which we become aware of the essence of beings as will to power through the complete emptying of all beings in the age of technology.

The four terms are unified in the *justice* that watches over their reciprocal strife. The importance of this fivefold in Heidegger's Nietzsche essay stems from the fact that it is so much better articulated than his fourfold in 1949. In the latter case, we have to make several tricky deductions to grasp what Heidegger is saying. But in the case of Nietzsche's metaphysics, Heidegger makes perfectly clear what the two axes of division are: *as such* versus *as a whole*, and *beings themselves* versus *beings in their history* (in their truth or openness). We can summarize the key terms in the form of a table:

eternal return	beings themselves, as a whole
will to power	beings themselves, as such
superman	beings in their openness, as a whole
nihilism	beings in their openness, as such

Justice is simply the fifth term, governing the interplay of the four. Heidegger left us no treatise on justice explaining exactly how the four terms would interact, just as he never spelled out the dynamics of the fourfold, or described exactly how the strife between earth and world unfolds in the artwork. He seems to have left this work for philosophers of the future ("the ones to come," perhaps). Yet he leaves no doubt that this quadruple structure is the final, most mature statement of his revolution in philosophy.

8

Strange Masterpiece in Bremen

One of the more legitimate games played by Heidegger scholars is to guess which of the philosopher's works deserves to be called his second *magnum opus* (no one doubts that *Being and Time* is his first). Many conservative Heideggerians nominate *Contributions to Philosophy* as their candidate for the second masterpiece, a judgment with which I cannot agree. Rüdiger Safranski, the most detailed biographer of Heidegger so far, nominates the 1929–30 lecture course on boredom and animal life. But however fascinating that course may be, it is more a lovely unfinished symphony than a true masterpiece.

For my own part, I have no doubt that the second great work of Heidegger is the seventy-page lecture *Einblick in das, was ist* (*Insight Into What Is*), first delivered in Bremen on December 1, 1949. The reader is advised that this is a minority view; indeed, I have never heard even one other person suggest it. Nonetheless, I am willing to place heavy bets that mainstream opinion will gradually come around to the same view. For this reason, *Being and Time* and *Insight Into What Is* are the only two works that I have given entire chapters of their own in this book, and I have even made sure to write the two chapters simultaneously. Although these works are separated by more than two decades, they belong together, just as the distant Everest and K2 are coupled in the fantasy life of mountaineers.

There is compelling circumstantial evidence for the importance of the Bremen lecture. *Insight Into What Is* was the first public lecture that Heidegger gave after World War II, and his first appearance on the stage following the Denazification process and the philosopher's resulting psychological problems. For Heidegger as for most Germans of his era, 1945 was a natural breaking point, splitting his life into before and after. *Insight Into What Is* counts as Heidegger's first piece of serious philosophy from the "after" period. To his credit, he had weathered the storms of the postwar period well enough to give us something truly new in his thinking. Many of Heidegger's best later essays ("The Thing," "Building Dwelling Thinking," and "The Question Concerning Technology") stem directly from this eerie 1949 lecture, which remained unpublished until 1994, and is still not available in full in English.

BREMEN

Bremen is an impressive northern German city that played a key role in the old Hanseatic League of medieval trading powers. Even now, Bremen (like Hamburg) remains a "free city" not belonging to any of the German states. Its architecture still reminds us of its proud past, with a stunning Old City Hall that transports awed visitors back to the age of the Viking invasions. Yet Bremen has never enjoyed the same degree of intellectual prestige as many German cities. The University of Bremen was founded only in recent decades, and the literary and philosophical reputation of the city cannot compare with those of Freiburg, Tübingen, Marburg, Göttingen, Leipzig, Dresden, and numerous other places.

Heidegger's link to the city arose from a pure accident. His admiring young student, the future cultural historian Heinrich Wiegand Petzet, came from a prominent Bremen family, and hit upon the unlikely idea of inviting Heidegger to lecture in this city of shipping merchants. Heidegger reacted warmly to the idea, and visited Bremen at an early date to repeat his 1930 lecture "On the Essence of Truth," which we discussed earlier. But this first visit was merely a warm-up for December 1949. It was then, in the New City Hall, that Heidegger presented one of the strangest jewels in all of Western philosophy.

DISTANCE AND NEARNESS

The lecture begins on a gripping contemporary note. According to Heidegger, all distances in time and space are shrinking. The new forms of modern technology destroy all former distances and make everything in the world available in an instant. But this does not give us true nearness to things. A small separation is not yet nearness, and a large separation is not yet distance.

As we have seen, both the critique of technology and the play of distance and nearness were foreshadowed in the final Marburg lecture course. In 1949, Heidegger takes a controversial further step in those immediate post-Hiroshima years: he argues that human beings gaze in horror at the explosion of the atomic bomb, but fail to realize that the true catastrophe happened long ago. The startling discovery of nuclear energy is nothing more than a surface incident compared to the deeper desolation of the history of being, in which being is progressively reduced to presence. Yet the real innovation of the Bremen lectures, a breakthrough so strange that it remains largely ignored even today, is Heidegger's concept of the *fourfold*. It was in Bremen that Heidegger first described the world as a mirror-play of earth, sky, gods, and mortals. Widely dismissed as meaningless or as hopelessly obscure, the fourfold is far too important to Heidegger for these dismissive interpretations to succeed.

The Thing

Heidegger has already suggested that inventions such as airplanes and telephones do not give us true nearness. This leads him to ask what nearness really means. What is near to us are things, but no one really knows what a thing is. Many theories have been given about this topic, but so far no one has thought about the thing *as* thing. Heidegger tries to do nothing less than this, using the example of a jug.

What is a jug? It is not only a container, but a container that stands independently in itself. In other words, it is not our perception of a jug that contains liquid, but the jug itself. Heidegger draws a distinction between objects and things. "Object" is a negative term, used to describe entities only in their presence-at-hand. But "thing" is a positive term referring to entities in their proper reality. The jug is not just an object, since it remains a container whether we look at it or not. Although this was already true of equipment in Heidegger's early writings, the emphasis in that period was on the need for human Dasein to be present for any reality to exist at all: without Dasein, there would be no truth and no world. By 1949, Heidegger's thinking about things had shifted in a subtle way. He now emphasizes that the thinghood of the jug is not dependent on whether Dasein looks at it or not.

The same holds for the fact that the jug must be *produced*. Obviously, without humans the jug would never have been built in the first place. But this does not mean that the thinghood of the jug is something human. Once it has been produced, the jug is free of its producer and stands in itself; even the producer who built it no longer has full control of it, and of course the jug continues to exist even when the producer is dead. In Heidegger's words, the jug is not a jug because it was produced, but rather is produced because it is a jug. The producer who builds the jug is only concerned with the thing's outward appearance, not its independent thinghood—after all, it is the jug that holds water or wine, not the potter.

Heidegger now makes a radical claim about the history of philosophy: Plato, Aristotle, and all later thinkers failed to think the true independent thinghood of the thing. All of them reduced things to something produced, or represented from the outside. Insofar as Heidegger sees his notion of the thinghood of things as a decisive rupture with the entire history of philosophy, it clearly deserves to be more central to the interpretation of his writings than it has been so far. In some ways, the thing is Heidegger's most important idea, one that encapsulates all the insights of his long career.

More on the Jug

The jug is a container. It is able to contain something because of a nothingness or empty space lying between the sides. What the potter really does is give shape to an emptiness that takes the liquid and holds it in place. Science would tell us that the jug is not actually empty, since it must be filled with air molecules or electromagnetic vibrations such as light. But Heidegger always holds that scientific explanations of things reduce them to presence, since they define things in terms of physical properties. The jug that holds and pours the wine is reduced by science to nonexistence; science sees the acts of holding and pouring as later properties that arise from the underlying reality of physical matter. In this way, science destroyed the thing long before the atom bomb made all things vulnerable.

For Heidegger, the explosions at Hiroshima and Nagasaki are merely a crude confirmation of what happened to the thing long ago. This is one of Heidegger's most typical gestures: he is always dismissive of the sorts of events that fill the newspapers, even major events such as the annihilation of two cities, because he thinks that true history unfolds on a much deeper level than the newspapers can ever grasp. By the same token, the jug always inhabits a much deeper level than what we see of it. The jug is not a mass of physical atoms, quarks, or subatomic strings. Before all this, it is something that gives and pours: in this way, the jug can also be called a gift.

THE FOURFOLD

This brings us to Heidegger's least understood and most neglected major concept: *the fourfold*. Whereas Plato, Aristotle, and all later thinkers failed to notice the thinghood of things, Heidegger tells us that this neglected thinghood has a fourfold structure. It is a fourfold of earth and sky, gods and mortals. Each of these four terms is given a poetic description that helps us very little in understanding their role in Heidegger's philosophy. We also hear that the thing is a "mirror-play" or "wedding" of all four terms, which reflect one another at all times in all places. In Heidegger's strange but wonderful phrase: "the thing things." The thing is an event that gathers the four, each of them mirroring the others. The thing is a unity of the four, and this unity can also be called *world*. "The world worlds," reminding us of the young Heidegger's phrase "it's worlding." The four terms are not present-at-hand, side by side, but belong together in an enclosing ring, or a dance.

Heideggerians have been so baffled by this strange fourfold that they usually ignore it completely. Most books on Heidegger either never mention the concept, or at most devote a few embarrassed paragraphs to it amidst hundreds of pages on other topics. Of the handful of weak attempts to understand the fourfold so far, most of them either dismiss it as a poetic tribute to Hölderlin (who did speak of all four terms in his poems at various times) or else claim that the number four is irrelevant, since all Heidegger means is that there is a "multiplicity" in the heart of being. According to this view, Heidegger could just as easily have spoken of an eight-fold or a fifteenfold.

This attitude by Heidegger scholars is irresponsible. Whether we understand the fourfold or not, it is clearly central to the philosopher's later writings. When Heidegger announces that Plato, Aristotle, and all later thinkers have failed to think the essence of the thing, he is claiming to set the stage for a revolution in philosophy based on a proper understanding of thinghood, and this revolution clearly pertains to the fourfold and nothing else. Furthermore, he does not drop the concept forever after giving a single lecture in Bremen. The fourfold seeps through all his later writings in one form or another. It is a scandal of Heidegger studies that more attention has not been paid to the mirror-play of the four. Here, I would like to venture a brief interpretation of the fourfold. This interpretation cannot even be called a "minority view," since other serious efforts have barely even been made. But since the readers of this book have already followed me through the fivefold of "Nietzsche's Metaphysics," what follows here will not come as much of a surprise.

Interpreting the Fourfold

First, it is obvious that the four terms of the fourfold (earth, sky, gods, and mortals) cannot be referring to distinct *kinds* of objects. Heidegger has already said that each of the four terms mirrors all the others simultaneously. This means that the four terms are structures belonging to all things, not four separate types of things. It would be charmingly naive for any philosopher to say: "there are four kinds of things in the world—gods, people, things way up in the sky, and things low down on the ground." For Heidegger, this sort of Kindergarten metaphysics would be even more impossible than for other philosophers, since he above all others despises any "ontic" classification of the world that would speak about kinds of beings rather than being itself. Heidegger's four are present at all times in all things, though they may be more concealed in some cases than in others.

Second, there is only one rigorous way to arrive at any fourfold structure in philosophy, and that is from the intersection of two distinct dualisms. For example, if we say that all humans are either male or female, and either right-handed or left-handed, we now have an efficient "fourfold" of our own: right-handed men, right-handed women, left-handed women, left-handed men. In Heidegger's case, all that we need to do is discover which two dualisms are at work, and the terms of the fourfold will immediately become clear, even if their "mirror-play" or the mechanics of their interaction might not.

It is actually not so difficult to discover which two dualisms are in play here. One opposition recurs throughout Heidegger's philosophy so repetitively that it often seems like the only idea he ever had: the distinction between a thing's shadowy concealment and its explicit appearance. This is also known as the temporal interplay between past and future, or between the equipment that silently functions and the signs and broken equipment that show themselves "as" what they are. Even in the fourfold of 1949, it is quite easy to split up the terms along these lines. Ever since the essay on artworks in the 1930s, Heidegger used "earth" as a term for mysterious concealment that withdraws from all appearance. By contrast, "sky" is defined in terms of specific visible examples such as the cycling of the seasons and the course of the planets and stars.

It is just as easy to classify the other two terms. Heidegger tells us that "gods" are never visible, but merely hint, making it clear that gods belong with earth on the side of concealment. Meanwhile, "mortals" are defined as the ones capable of death *as* death, putting mortals on the side of clearing or revealing, due to the role of the explicit as-structure here. Mortals and sky, then, are terms of "future" or of the revealed realm, whereas earth and gods belong to "past" or the concealed realm.

This still leaves us with the burden of finding a second principle of opposition. Although somewhat trickier, this also turns out not to be so difficult. It hinges on the difference between the unity of a thing's existence and the plurality of its essence or qualities. If we look at the concealed realm, we find that Heidegger always defines earth as a single, unified, sheltering force into which everything withdraws. Earth never has any parts for Heidegger, but is always one earth. By contrast, the gods are plural, and all of them hint individually.

If we now turn our attention to the cleared or revealed side of the world, sky (despite being singular in terms of grammar) is obviously a plural term, since unlike earth it is defined through numerous specific examples. By contrast, mortals are engaged with *death*, and we know from elsewhere in Heidegger's writings that death or Angst reveals the world as a whole, and not a plurality of specific things.

This second axis is in fact quite similar to the classical distinction between existence and essence. It is also closely linked to a famous distinction in Husserl between a phenomenon having a specific essence (such as being catlike or grey) and the fact that it is a phenomenon in the first place. As the young Heidegger put it, every entity in the world is both something *specific*, and something *at all*. This gives us the following summary of the fourfold, along with the corresponding terms from the earlier treatise on Nietzsche's metaphysics:

Earth	concealed	something at all [eternal return]
Gods	concealed	something specific [will to power]
Mortals	revealed	something at all [superman]
Sky	revealed	something specific [nihilism]

In my view, no more than this can be clearly determined from Heidegger's own writings—but also no less.

The next step would be to explain how the "mirroring" process works, how any of these terms could possibly reflect the others, and how the fourfolds of two separate objects affect one another when they interact. But this would take us beyond Heidegger's own writings, and hence would be inappropriate for an introductory book of this kind. Already, we have needed to do plenty of interpretation merely to make sense of the four terms, since Heidegger never does this for us explicitly.

Heidegger was never a great fan of the Romans, and often criticized the Latin language and Latin thought for reducing reality to human *access* to it. The long decay of reality into mere human access to reality leads, he says, to the philosophy of Kant, in which things are entirely reduced to objects of human representation. This is a remarkable change in Heidegger's self-understanding compared with his earlier attitude. When Kant speaks of the "thing in itself," what he means in Heideggerian terms is "object in itself," not things that stand in themselves the way the jug does. But the object in itself gives us no true nearness to the things. Today, everything is equally near and far. True nearness actually comes only from the fourfold. "The thing things," and in this way brings the four to one another without erasing their distance from one another. Heidegger says that we can only see this by stepping away from the kind of thinking that represents things as objects, and toward the kind that he calls "commemorative thinking" or "meditative thinking." These bulky-sounding terms simply refer to a kind of thinking that does not represent things as objects viewed from the outside, but points toward their mysterious inwardness as unique events. In the early lecture courses, he had called this process "formal indication," but now gives it a more poetic title.

The Enframing

The mastery of distance does not bring us near to things. True nearness comes only when "the thing things," when it sets the unity of the fourfold into motion. Paradoxically, this must happen at all times, but at some times more than others. If we leave our house and stroll beneath the shade of a tree, the real distance between the house and the tree is not based on a physical measurement, but on how intimately or distantly these concern us, as was already seen in the analysis of space in *Being and Time*. Distance and nearness are not objective physical terms, but refer to how close or far we are from the essence of things. Being able to fly from New York to London in a few hours by supersonic jet obviously does not mean that we are more closely in contact with the essence of British culture than one hundred years ago. Even the shallowest poseurs can fly to Heathrow Airport, but some impoverished scholar on a remote continent might grasp the inner reality of Britain quite deeply without being able to afford a visit there.

In our time we have fallen under the reign of scientific representation, which has no respect for the distance of things from us. We have entered a world of sheer presence that reduces things to objects of calculation. Everything becomes equally indifferent and equally valid. Everything in our world turns into nothing but a stockpile or standing reserve. Everything is reduced to its utility. True enough, carpenters always build their tables for some purpose, just as farmers put their livestock in one place rather than another for a specific reason. But what happens in our own time is something far worse than this. Land is no longer respected in its own right, but is organized and arranged in a certain way in order to extract coal or metallic ore: land is reduced to a mining district. (As a left-wing Swiss activist once joked, land now exists in Zürich only to prevent banks from falling to the center of the earth and melting.) The Rhine is no longer the mysterious river written about in Hölderlin's poems, since (as Heidegger hilariously puts it) the Rhine is now "a site on call for inspection by vacationers ordered there by the tourist industry." Farming is no longer what it always was, but has become a mechanized nourishment business. Controversially, though predictably, Heidegger says that mechanized farming is essentially no different from the production of corpses in gas chambers, the blockading and starving of nations, or the manufacture of hydrogen bombs.

It is true that some of these things are generally seen as efficient and useful, while others are viewed as inhumane monstrosities. But for Heidegger, the "essence" in all cases is the same. All of them reduce the things of the world to stockpiled presence-at-hand, just as the history of philosophy since ancient Greece has reduced the world to presence. The damnable atrocities of the past century are the result of a metaphysics of presence that began a long time ago, and give us nothing more than its logical outcome. For Heidegger, databanks and mass-produced shoes are essentially the same as Auschwitz, Hiroshima, or Verdun.

Unlike a jug, minerals lying in the ground do not need to be produced by humans. Even so, they are ordered and arranged by humans for the purpose of generating heat. A hydroelectric plant is placed in a stream, and its turbines are spun by water pressure; this motion is converted into electrical current, which is then extended across a large-scale power grid. None of these things comes to presence unless this has already been ordered or arranged for some purpose. But where does this system of purposes come to an end? In *Being and Time*, the system of tools ended in Dasein's "for-the-sake-of-which," meaning that all tools gained their meaning from Dasein's own being. In modern technology, however, the chain *never* comes to an end. There is no purpose; everything feeds on itself, moving in an endless vicious circle. Technology exists for the sake of technology, feeding endlessly on itself. The earth is now plundered for its coal, ore, crude oil, and fish.

Strangely enough, Heidegger does not believe that humans are to blame for this horrible predicament—instead, being itself is to blame! For it is being that passes itself off as mere presence, and thereby invites us to convert things into a stockpile of manipulable slag. It is not just inanimate objects that become standing reserve, but humans as well. We are all reduced to the status of crude oil or coal. This is true not only when we are exterminated in death camps or blown up by mass-produced bombs, but even when we are simply "treated as numbers" by university administrators, telemarketers, or military draft boards.

All this ordering of stockpiles has only one goal: to treat the whole of presence as a standing reserve. The system of ordering is not made up of all individual human purposes, but is something deeper than all of them. Heidegger's name for the entire system of stockpiled present-at-hand things is the *enframing*. The German word is *Gestell*, a normal everyday word meaning a rack used for hanging clothes or umbrellas. But Heidegger's *Gestell* is a rack not just for umbrellas, but for everything that exists. All of nature and all of history are hung out to dry on this global rack, all perfectly arranged, stripped of all mystery. This enframing is the essence of technology. Most people believe that modern technology is composed of machines, but in fact, machines are built only because they serve the enframing. A machine is not just a more efficient replacement for the former tools and utensils. At least these former tools each belonged to a specific place of its own. By contrast, the enframing has bulldozed all the old places and established an entirely new grid of utter desolation. The essence of technology is not something technical. All attempts to manage technology by technical means will fail, just as mathematicians cannot grasp the essence of mathematics with equations, and just as the essence of history cannot be grasped by giving a history of historians. Only philosophical thinking (commemorative thinking) is strong enough for this crucial task.

While a jug is meant to stand in itself, a truck exists only insofar as it ordered for some other purpose and remains constantly in circulation. Machine parts are not really parts, since they are completely interchangeable with other such parts, meaning that they are completely reduced to their outward look or outward usefulness. Today's forester no longer resembles his grandfather: today, foresters are ordered by the lumber industry to produce paper for newspapers and mass magazines, which give us gossip and mere information rather than any nearness to things. If all radios were taken away from humans, they would be faced with infinite boredom and emptiness, since humans have now been reduced to the stockpiled puppets of worldwide enframing. Although most people try to explain technology as a product of human intelligence, the reverse is actually true: just as philosophy reduces things to representations, technology reduces things to standing reserve.

It might seem that there are limits to the essence of technology. After all, there is also nature, which sets clear boundaries to our manipulation: we remain helpless before tsunamis and hurricanes, and our infrastructure sometimes collapses even during ice storms. Yet consider how it is that humans really see nature. Our view of nature comes from natural science, which conceives nature only as a representation or standing reserve. Physics sees nature as a stockpile of matter and energy, reducing all its other qualities (their colors, odors, and specific histories) to meaningless residue. It is no accident that modern technology and modern physics were born together, since both are champions of stockpile and enframing. Modern technology is not an application of modern science; rather, science is already ordered in advance by technology. Modern atomic physics is essentially no different from all other modern science. Here as everywhere else in the modern world, nature no longer serves as any kind of barrier to technology.

The Danger

All true nearness is nearness through the concealed mirror-play of the fourfold. When this nearness is withheld, reduced to presence, then we have the enframing. The enframing happens because it does not preserve the thing as thing, just as Plato, Aristotle, and all later thinkers did not. The enframing does not protect the thing, or take custody of it in any way. The thing as thing is neglected: according to Heidegger this is not a judgmental statement, given that it is not humans who do this, but being itself. When the thing is neglected, then the world is not world. World means the thinging of the thing, in its ambiguous status as both openly visible and sheltered in darkness. The worlding of world is an event, in a sense of the term that we have barely begun to grasp. When we do finally grasp it, we will be able to overcome the nihilism that has reduced the world to a lethal playground of industrial wastelands and nuclear bombs.

The world is both visible ("cleared") and hidden, and this is the meaning of the Greek word for truth: *aletheia*. But *aletheia* is not something under human control, since unconcealment always requires concealment as well. Truth is the "sending" of being in different forms by being itself, which gives us a series of different epochs of the history of being, each with its own special features. Humans are distracted by whatever is visibly present. Being and truth are both forgotten, since both withdraw from human access and leave us only with what is present. The era when the withdrawal of being reaches completion is the era to which we now belong: the epoch of enframing. But even so, a distant ray of hope appears in the enframing. For being itself can also be called *the danger*—since it contains the possibility of "errance," or error. And for Heidegger, as for his beloved poet Hölderlin, danger and saving power are always two sides of the same coin.

Error is not just accidental, but belongs to the very essence of truth as unconcealment, since nothing can ever be completely unconcealed. Danger conceals itself from us. It leads to distress, and those moments when we seem to be without any distress may in fact be the most serious form of distress of all. With remarkable insensitivity, Heidegger now asks rhetorically whether the victims of mass death really die. His unspoken answer is "no." We can only say that the victims of mass death "lose their lives," because to die means to carry out death in its very essence (which the slain of Auschwitz, Hiroshima, and Verdun were presumably unable to accomplish). Not all humans are mortals.

According to Heidegger, everyone tries to think of technology in technological terms, but this is not sufficient. Everyone remains equally confused: those who praise technology, those who denounce it, and those who claim it is inherently neutral and only becomes good or bad depending on the use that is made of it. All three of these views misrepresent technology, since all think it is only a means to an end. In fact, the essence of technology lies far deeper than the superficial realm of means and purposes. Presence has become the basic trait of the contemporary world, just as it blinded the history of philosophy since ancient Greece. The danger is the enframing: not as technological machinery, but as one of the two faces of being itself.

The Turn

We are not aware of the full danger as we go about reducing the entities of the world to stockpiles of presence, even if it sometimes causes us to feel depression or anguish. We should not think of history as a series of newsworthy occurrences, but instead as the way that being sends itself to us. In our epoch, being sends itself in the shape of technology. But this epoch is beyond human control, and cannot simply be mastered by human political deeds such as meetings, United Nations conferences, or improved legal systems. Humans are not the lords of being. Nonetheless, humans are still the *shepherds* of being. We are not completely helpless in the face of enframing or the stockpiled standing reserve. In fact, Heidegger holds that the essence of being *needs* us, for without us it will never come to presence as what it is. But for this to happen, humans must first open themselves to the essence of technology.

We humans are not capable of essential resistance to the current desolate epoch of being. But at least we can think, and thinking is the most authentic form of acting. This requires a new and special relation to language. Without such a relation to language, everything remains an aimless deliberation about one topic or another. Language is not simply the expression of thoughts that already exist in our minds beforehand. Instead, language is the primary dimension in which humans are able to respond or correspond to being and its claim on us. Only by thinking do we learn to overcome enframing. Being itself is the danger, and for this reason it turns against itself in forgetfulness. Yet danger includes the possibility of a turn in which our forgetfulness of being could suddenly veer toward the truth of being. Such a turn requires that the danger become explicitly present as the danger that it is. Heidegger suggests that we may already stand in the first shadows of this approaching turn. No one knows when and how it will happen, and it is not even necessary for us to know. Indeed, it would actually be a bad thing to know in advance when the turn is coming, since we humans are the shepherds of being. As shepherds, we are meant to wait.

One of the most frequently quoted passages from Hölderlin's poetry is the phrase "where the danger is, there too lies the saving power." Heidegger and his followers take pleasure in citing this phrase as often as possible whenever technology is mentioned. Danger and saving power are not two different things that lie side by side. Instead, they are two faces of being itself. Danger is both everywhere and nowhere, and comes from our entire epoch of technological enframing. But once the danger appears openly *as* danger, we will see that our forgetting of being was not just an unlucky negative event, but also a way for being to remain sheltered and hidden. The turn will happen suddenly, as the clearing of being. Heidegger calls this sudden turn a lightning-flash.

His Bremen lecture is entitled *Insight Into What Is*, and "what is" is not any specific entity, but rather being itself. Heidegger now makes a play on words between *Einblick* (insight) and his newly coined word *Einblitz* (which we might call "enlightenment," to keep the sense of lightning from the German word *Blitz*). The enlightening of the world will be the flash of being itself into a world forsaken by technology. In other words, "insight into what is" does not just refer to an insight that we humans gain while listening to a strange lecture in Bremen. It actually refers to a turn that happens in being itself. In closing, Heidegger asks if we can already see the lightning-flash of being in the danger of technology. If everything is laid waste by death camps, atom bombs, strip mines, and mechanized farms, this is no reason for despair. By reaching this point of danger, the enframing may suddenly turn into the saving power. As the shepherds of being, we humans can only think—and wait.

9

The Task of Thinking

The Bremen lecture had a distinctly eerie tone, and this strangeness did not disappear in Heidegger's remaining productive years. His works from 1950 onward are as disturbingly poetic as those of a cutting-edge dance troupe or theater company. The mirror-play of the fourfold continues to dominate his thought in various ways. This was also a period during which Heidegger regained a good deal of his international popularity. Having slipped in the 1930s into the shame of the Third Reich, and regarded by some critics as a spent force, Heidegger managed to reinvent himself with a new voice, with a new public image as an elderly sage in dark times. While many would never forgive his political disaster, for the most part he received a warm welcome in his return to the philosophical world.

1950: Language Speaks

In 1950, Heidegger gave a lecture with the simple title "Language." It is not contained in the English version of *On the Way to Language*, which is merely an abridged edition of the German book. While those who wish to learn more about Heidegger's ideas on language can profit from the other essays contained in the English translation, the "Language" essay has always struck me as the most interesting of them all.

Humans always speak, says Heidegger. We speak even when we say, hear, or read nothing at all, and even when we sleep. By this he means that humans must always interpret and articulate the world in some specific way, even when no words are used. It is only language that makes humans what they are; animals have no language. But in fact, it is not humans who speak: *language speaks*. In Heidegger's view, to regard language as a human activity would be every bit as shallow as to think that technology comes from machines built by humans. Just as technology is the face of being itself as presence, language is being viewed as *the interplay of world and thing*. For much of the past century, the philosophy of language has been the dominant branch of philosophy, and on this basis efforts have been made to see Heidegger as a philosopher of language. This effort is doomed to fail. Heidegger has no interest at all in language as the way that humans gain access to the world. He is interested in language as an element of the world itself, or of being itself. If Heidegger is a philosopher of language, this is only because he is a philosopher of *world and thing*: of the mirror-play of the fourfold.

A Winter Evening

To begin to approach the essence of language, Heidegger considers poetry, which he regards as the purest form of speaking. The poem he chooses to discuss is "A Winter Evening," by the lurid Austrian genius Georg Trakl (1887–1914), a master of morbid imagery who died of an overdose of cocaine. It might be translated as follows:

A Winter Evening

When the snow falls at the pane,
evening bells will long resound—
the table set for many guests
in a well-provided house.

Some, along their wandering,
follow dark roads to the gate.
Cooling juices from the earth
will feed the golden tree of grace.

Silent drifter steps inside,
a painful threshold turned to stone.
There, in purest brightness shine,
on the table, bread and wine.

Trakl's poem speaks of numerous alluring things: snow, bell, window, pain, threshold, falling, and resounding. By naming these entities, the poem is not just giving titles to things that are already found present-at-hand. Instead, it calls these things before us for the first time. This calling summons the objects into a true nearness, which (we already know) is also a kind of distance.

The presence of these things in the poem is something much deeper than the presence of physical bells or snowflakes lying before us. If I were to see a snow-covered bell in my front yard, I might simply represent it as a set of visible qualities. But if a bell is named in the poem, it is summoned before me in a presence that is simultaneously an absence. In the poem, the thing things: *the bell bells*, to use a phrase that Heidegger himself never uses. In this way, the bell is gathered into the mirror-play of the fourfold of earth and sky, gods and mortals. The bell unites the fourfold even though the four poles remain distinct. This united fourfold is the world.

WORLD AND THING

For Heidegger, world no longer means the unity of nature and history, nor something created by God, nor even the sum of all present-at-hand things. Instead, the world is a summoning that relates world to thing and thing to world. World and thing do not stand next to each other as separate realities, but interpenetrate one another. They are unified without melting together, in a middle ground that Heidegger calls "the between." Language is nothing other than this between. The between is also called "the difference." Heidegger had written years earlier of the ontological difference between being and specific beings. Then as now, being and beings are not separate, but interpenetrate one another and meet in a middle ground.

This difference bears the world in its worlding, and things in their thinging. It is this difference in which world and thing turn toward one another: the difference is the event in which world and thing correspond to one another. Other key words in Trakl's poem are "pain" and "threshold." The difference between world and thing is the threshold where they meet. Pain is the crack that reveals to us to the tear that splits world and thing from each other. The calling that occurs in poetic language is the summoning of the intimate relation of world and thing—and true intimacy always requires that intimate things remain distinct despite their close-ness. Heidegger says that difference shelters the thing in the calm of the fourfold. Continuing to develop the strange terminology of the essay, Heidegger says that to shelter or protect something in this calm means to give peace or silence to world and thing in their relation to one another. The gathering can be referred to as a "sounding," which Heidegger (not surprisingly) distinguishes from all present-at-hand transmission of sound. Putting these two thoughts together, Heidegger says that language speaks because language is the sounding of the silence of the fourfold. As the reader may already have guessed, this essay is generally regarded as one of Heidegger's strangest.

1951–52: We Are Still Not Thinking

In the winter semester of 1951–52, Heidegger was finally allowed to lecture again at the University of Freiburg, six years after the end of the war. It would be his final official lecture course. His swan song was the widely popular work known in English as *What Is Called Thinking?* Heidegger begins by saying that we learn to think only by thinking, just as we learn to swim only by swimming. Yet the most thought-provoking thing in our time is that we are still not thinking. He claims that this remark applies to himself no less than to others, and also insists that it is not the fault of humans that they are not yet thinking. Being itself is to blame, just as being itself is to blame for the rampage of global technology. The fact that we are not yet thinking is not the result of World War II or the atom bomb, but goes all the way back to the dawn of history. What is most thought-provoking is being, and being always con-ceals itself.

Science and Thinking

Science does not think. This statement is bound to annoy scientists despite Heidegger's unconvincing claim that it is not meant as a criticism. Whether critical or not, it is certainly not a new idea for Heidegger in 1951. From the start of his career, Heidegger saw science as a kind of external representation or calculation that reduces things to their utility or their measurability by humans. To use Heidegger's terminology from 1919, science interprets things as occurrences, not as events. This is why science does not think.

Drawing a pessimistic conclusion from this idea, Heidegger states dismissively that it is a waste of time to attempt dialogues between scientists and thinkers. Science deals with what is accessible, but thought is concerned with whatever withdraws from all access.

We find an analogy to the thinker in the old-fashioned carpenter, who deals with wood as a genuine thing in which numerous forms are sleeping. But it is now quite different for the worker in an industrial table factory, who merely throws a switch and achieves profitable results, never coming to grips at all with the withdrawn forces lying in the wood. In America and elsewhere, thinking has been reduced to calculation or logistics. The Anglo-Saxon countries are the lands of industry and one-track thinking. (The same goes without saying for Soviet communism, which Heidegger detested even more than the Anglophone world.) Language has been reduced to a series of cute abbreviations that fail to capture the dignity of the things to which they refer. "University" becomes *Uni* in German or U. in English, so that the University of Texas becomes "UT," just as "political science" becomes "poli. sci." Heidegger regards this apparently harmless process as deeply sinister, since it degrades the things whose names are abbreviated. To take another example, one of Kant's most famous terms for human consciousness is "the transcendental unity of apperception," and some Kant scholars now simplify this concept by calling it "the TUA." While this abbreviation is annoying enough for most of us, it would have enraged Heidegger beyond all measure.

THE HISTORY OF PHILOSOPHY

In one of his more unusual historical claims, Heidegger says that one of the secret dominant philosophers of our time is the German thinker Arthur Schopenhauer (1788–1860). Schopenhauer is known for his great influence on Nietzsche and the composer Richard Wagner, and is widely respected for his brilliant literary style. Yet he is most often viewed as a prickly maverick or crank lying just outside the mainstream of the history of philosophy. Heidegger (who rarely speaks of Schopenhauer elsewhere) says that this is incorrect. Schopenhauer secretly influences all contemporary philosophy through his notion that "the world is my idea." In other words, the world exists as my representation, or as an outward appearance. (This is actually only half the story, since Schopenhauer also views the world as a dark subterranean *will* that causes suffering.) In this way, Schopenhauer does not let the things stand in themselves, and others have followed him in this belief.

Heidegger follows with a long analysis of Schopenhauer's greatest admirer, Nietzsche, that need not be repeated here. It focuses on Nietzsche's idea of eternal return, and on the superman who would be strong enough to bear it. Heidegger now says that the eternal return is Nietzsche's one great thought. Every great thinker has just one great thought—one deep and inexhaustible thought. This seems even more true of Heidegger himself than of most philosophers. By contrast, scientific researchers all discover numerous different results, which Heidegger does not regard as a good thing. To respect a philosophy is to take hold of its one great thought and never let it go. Nor does this always require accurate historical knowledge. For instance, Heidegger claims that he would have given Kant a grade of "F" for his unskilled interpretations of Plato and Aristotle, but even so, it was Kant who creatively transformed Plato's philosophy more than anyone else. Only the greatest thinkers can truly be influenced by other great thinkers. Mediocre thinkers are stuck with what Heidegger calls "constipated originality," and the ideas that they believe are new are really just regurgitations of the deep insights of greater thinkers.

THINKING AND THANKING

Returning to the main theme of the course, Heidegger says that his phrase "being and time" points to something that was unthought in all previous metaphysics. In German, the title "What Is Called Thinking?" is ambiguous. It can also be translated just as accurately as "What Calls For Thinking?"—in other words, what is most thought provoking? Humans did not create being; we are the shepherds of being, not its lords. Being is a gift. Hence, thinking is also a kind of *thanking* (the two words are just as similar in German as in English: *denken/danken*). We cannot receive the hints that emanate from the hidden region of being unless we are already listening in that direction. This is done neither by science nor by logic, which reduce being to the way it is represented by humans, deaf to any mystery of being. By contrast, the great thinking of the Greeks was nonconceptual, since what is mysterious can never be reduced to concepts.

The early Greek philosopher Parmenides said that "being is." This sounds trivial. It remains trivial as long as we regard being as nothing more than something present in the world: for *of course* being is. What else would it be? But for the kind of thinking that Heidegger urges, the "is" remains a mystery. It refers to a swirling, turbulent absence from visibility that can never be clearly defined. Everything that appears must have arisen from a deeper conceal- ment. The reason we are not yet thinking is because we are not yet able to do justice to the emergence of things from concealment. Thinking means letting things be, not reducing them to concepts or representations—as science, logic, and technology do. The best service that humans can render to being is to devote thought to the being of beings. And this means *thanking*: a gratitude to being as what is most thought provoking.

1955: Releasement

In 1955, Heidegger returned to Messkirch for a celebration hon- oring the minor composer Conradin Kreutzer (1780–1849), who was also a native of the town. Heidegger's short speech of less than twenty pages remarkably says nothing about Kreutzer's music. But it is famous for other reasons. It is in this speech that Heidegger speaks of releasement, which is often simply left in the German as *Gelassenheit*.

HOME AND SOIL

Heidegger wonders aloud whether it is really possible to speak in honor of someone who works with music. (He proves his wonder by barely speaking about Kreutzer at all.) More generally, the fact that we are talking does not mean that we are thinking. In our era, everyone talks more and more and seeks increasing amounts of information, yet everyone becomes more and more thoughtless. Humans today flee from thinking, even though it seems like we have become more educated than ever. Thinking has turned into sheer calculation and efficiency, even in cases (such as philosophy) where it rarely uses numbers. Thinking now jumps from one opportunity to the next, and never becomes reflective; it has lost its nourishing soil, and all great works must be rooted in soil. All great works, in every domain, need to spring from a home of some sort.

But if we are not thinking, Heidegger continues, perhaps this only means that our thinking is lying fallow, waiting to blossom forth. Humans are the thinking or reflecting creatures, and thought can rise up from even the simplest things that are close at hand. In order to think, one must rise from the deep soil of a homeland. But in 1955, many Germans have lost their homes and live in industrial wastelands. Even those lucky ones who still have their homes are perhaps even more homeless, since they are spellbound by the thoughtlessness of radio, film, and illustrated magazines. All these new media have become more real to humans than the natural course of day and night. The rootedness of humans in the earth is now deeply threatened. Heidegger speaks dismissively about an apparently prestigious meeting that took place that same year, in which eighteen Nobel Prize winners had assembled and issued a proclamation that modern natural science is a path toward a happier human life. For Heidegger this statement does not spring from a true reflection, since it misses the fact that humans have submitted to a calculative and technical thinking that first arose in the seventeenth century, and whose roots lie even deeper in the past.

Against Calculative Thinking

Nuclear power plants will soon be built all over the earth. Once this has happened, we will have reached a completely new stage in the reign of technology—and technology is neither something technical nor something human. No human commission or agency can bring the atomic age to a halt, since it is not of our creation. Even grimmer, in Heidegger's view, was a statement of that era by the American chemist Wendell Stanley. According to Stanley, the hour is near when life itself will be placed in the hands of chemists, who will be able to construct and alter living substances at will. For Heidegger, compared to this horrifying possibility, even the hydrogen bomb is nothing important. The powers of technology are becoming uncanny. But even more uncanny is that we humans are not prepared for any of these terrifying scientific advances, and do not think of them reflectively. Humans have not yet managed to counter calculative thinking with reflective thinking.

But Heidegger ends on a positive note. Perhaps we are nearer than we think to regaining contact with the soil. We cannot simply abandon radios, newspapers, and power plants. Yet perhaps while using these technical devices in our everyday lives, we can still say "no" to their attempt to claim our entire being. We need to say "yes" and "no" to technology simultaneously. To describe this mixed attitude, Heidegger revives an old German word: *releasement*. The meaning of the technical world is hidden. It is a secret, and like all secrets it both shows itself and withdraws at the same time.

Releasement to the things and openness to their secret belong together as two faces of the same attitude. If we can achieve this double attitude, it will give us a new rootedness in a soil where the creation of lasting works can take root. But in the meantime, humans will find themselves in a dangerous position on earth. We do not know how long this danger will last. The danger does not lie in a third world war (a very real possibility in 1955), since there would still be danger even if all threat of war were removed. The danger lies in a deeper desolation stemming from the essence of technology itself, which is nothing human, but belongs to the very essence of being. Being is danger because it always hides itself, and tempts us to conceive it as presence.

1963–64: The End of Philosophy

In 1964, Heidegger's short work "The End of Philosophy and the Task of Thinking" first appeared, in a French edition. It would be his last piece of great philosophy, published at age seventy-five. Since 1930, Heidegger says, he has made repeated attempts to rethink the central question of *Being and Time*. This now leads him to ask two questions. First, what does it mean if Heidegger says that philosophy has entered its final stage? Second, what task still remains for thinking as philosophy comes to an end?

METAPHYSICS IN THE BAD SENSE

When Heidegger says philosophy, what he means is metaphysics (in the bad sense of the term). Not only is metaphysics the attempt to think the whole of beings—even more importantly, it is always a kind of representational thinking, which reduces things to their presence in our minds. In metaphysics, all entities are shown to rest on some deeper ground or cause, and this ground is supposed to be more truly present in the world than everything that derives from it. It scarcely matters what philosophers think this ground is: it may be atoms that cause everything else; it may be God, the sole timeless and eternal entity; it may be Kant's conditions of possibility for all human experience; it may be will to power, as in Nietzsche's philosophy. The difference between all these theories does not matter for Heidegger. Despite their apparent disagreement, all such theories are equally rooted in presence, and show no sense for the secret that withdraws. Metaphysics always derives the presence of things from the ground that is responsible for them. Philosophy in this sense has reached its end, because it is now complete. Completion does not mean that philosophy has become more and more perfect over the years: Plato is not more perfect than Parmenides, Hegel not more perfect than Kant, and Nietzsche not more perfect than St. Thomas Aquinas. Every era of philosophy has its own necessity.

Metaphysics is Platonism, since Plato is the one who saw all entities as derivative the ideas or perfect forms, of which everything in our world is merely a shadow. The most radical modern philosophies, such as those of Nietzsche and Karl Marx, are nothing but reversals of Platonism that retain Plato's basic assumptions. And this is why philosophy is now complete. Wherever philosophy is still attempted, it is nothing but a superficial renaissance without any originality. It would show a lack of imagination, Heidegger believes, if we expected further philosophies of the previous type to keep emerging in the future. If philosophy is ending, this does not mean that it is simply disappearing—rather, it is turning into science.

SCIENCE

Although the sciences have become increasingly independent from philosophy, they originated from philosophy and remain intellectually dependent on it. Genetics, physics, geology, biology, and all other sciences are each a kind of specialized metaphysics, since each of them believes in certain fundamental realities from which everything else is derived. For example, for all of genetics, everything comes back to the DNA molecule, which serves as the ground for all more complicated phenomena, such as blue eyes or hereditary disease. And this, of course, is metaphysics in the bad sense. All sciences will soon become cybernetics, as all human activity will become completely planned and controlled. Western and European thinking has triumphed worldwide. Across the planet, all entities have been redefined as objects of technical manipulation, including human beings.

A TASK FOR THOUGHT

It is not yet clear (whether in 1964 or in 2007) if world civilization will be destroyed or will somehow become stabilized. In this situation, Heidegger wonders what task there might still be for thinking. He has a definite answer in mind, and says that the task of philosophy was already present in the Greek beginning, although it remained concealed. This does not entail an arrogant dismissal of the entire history of philosophy, since according to Heidegger we still need to consult the entire history of philosophy in order to pursue the new task.

He follows with a short but fascinating comparison between the philosophies of Husserl and Hegel. In some ways these two philosophers are as different as can be. But what both have in common is their assumption that reality means what is present for human consciousness. Both of them reduce things to representation, and for this reason both remain trapped in bad metaphysics. But Heidegger contends that the lucid appearance of phenomena in human consciousness would not be possible unless it happened in an "opening" or "clearing" of some sort. In this clearing, just as in a forest clearing, there is a perpetual war between light and shadow. Philosophy, which has reached its end, never paid any attention throughout its long history to this clearing of being. The Greeks already knew this when they defined truth as *aletheia*, which means an uncovering that always contains concealment as well. The path to *aletheia* or truth requires a completely new attitude. This leads Heidegger to yet another attempt to reformulate the central question of *Being and Time*: instead of the phrase "being and time," he now asks about the interrelation of "clearing and presence."

LOOKING BACK AT HIS YOUTH

We close this chapter by returning to an essay of one year earlier. In 1963, Heidegger contributed to a volume honoring the publisher Hermann Niemeyer, an important figure in the phenomenological movement who published key works by Husserl, Heidegger, Max Scheler, and others. His brief essay is entitled "My Way in Phenomenology." In less than ten pages, Heidegger charmingly reviews the early portions of his career, from his first year as a student in Freiburg on up to 1929. Since the current book has tried to interpret Heidegger as a radical phenomenologist, there is no better way for us to end than by reviewing Heidegger's path through phenomenology and beyond.

As a teenager, Heidegger had been given a copy of Franz Brentano's book on the manifold meaning of being in Aristotle. In a vague, half-conscious way, the adolescent Heidegger had wondered about the fundamental sense of being that would unify all its multiple meanings. Only as a university student did Heidegger come into contact with the works of Brentano's student, Edmund Husserl. He found Husserl's *Logical Investigations* in the library and was able to borrow its two volumes repeatedly, since no one else ever seemed to want them. He read these books again and again, deeply fascinated even though they did not relate as directly as he had hoped to the manifold meaning of being. In fact, he was not exactly sure what fascinated him so much about Husserl's book. But he was especially intrigued by the sixth logical investigation, which made the distinction between sensuous and categorial intuition. As we have seen, categorial intuition later became Heidegger's path toward the question of being. In any perception of green, table, zebra, or even the word "and," being is always silently present in the background as the deepest of all categories. Husserl had lost interest in his own sixth investigation by the time Heidegger met him, and even had to be pressured by his young friends to reprint it. Husserl then looked on, supportively but somewhat puzzled, as Heidegger covered this important investigation in his own lectures and seminars. These patient labors eventually led to the radical new form of phenomenology that we have covered in this book: Heidegger's own philosophy.

While doing all this work on Husserl, Heidegger eventually concluded that phenomenology's insistence on dealing with the things themselves rather than theories about things was grasped even more deeply by Greek philosophy as *aletheia*: truth, in the sense of unveiling. The Greeks understood what Husserl did not—that all light emerges only from shadow, and never entirely dispels that shadow. Things do not appear in lucid presence in consciousness, but emerge only partly from the unveiling of being. By 1963, phenomenology as a philosophical school seems to have run out of energy, and in Heidegger's opinion is now largely consigned to the history books. But it remains a real possibility for human Dasein, since phenomenology means a way of staying true to what must be thought. Phenomenology lives on, in altered form, in Heidegger's own call for thinking.

10

Heidegger's Legacy

As mentioned in the introduction, one piece of evidence for Heidegger's greatness is his continuing appeal beyond his most predictable circle of supporters. No one is very surprised when political leftists admire Noam Chomsky, when right-wingers adore Ayn Rand, when gays read Oscar Wilde, or when Marxists celebrate the art of Diego Rivera. The real test of historic greatness is the ability to appeal across the board to those who do not share one's political views, passport status, or common practical interests. This tends to become increasingly evident through the test of time, as the life-and-death struggles of any given era slowly fade. Today's aristocrats can admire the literary style of Julius Caesar without minding his demagogic politics too much; arch-supporters of today's Pope can still offer toasts to Dante's great poem and forget his long crusade against Vatican political power. By this criterion, Heidegger is doing quite well. Despite the grave blots on his political record, Heidegger is recognized as a great philosopher by many of his obvious natural enemies: Marxists, Jews, decadent artists, scientists, and Silicon Valley engineers. But perhaps even more telling is his growing reputation in the school known as analytic philosophy.

His Legacy Now

For most of the past century, there has been a strict institutional split between the styles of philosophy associated with the English-speaking world and Continental Europe. Anglo-American analytic philosophy is modeled on the natural sciences, and has sought to erase all vague, fuzzy works of metaphysics that are unwilling to define their key terms clearly. Like the sciences, analytic philosophy has an intellectual culture dominated by brief journal articles that try to make progress on narrowly defined technical issues. The lifestyle of analytic philosophy resembles that of the sciences in other ways as well: it is notable for aggressive oral debate, an admiration for its great figures that nonetheless loathes any form of worship, an insistence on the clearest possible language, and no tolerance at all for anything it regards as superstition or sloppy thinking.

Furthermore, though it does not entirely lack interest in the history of its discipline, analytic philosophy prefers to focus on the cutting-edge problems of today rather than becoming immersed in the philosophies of the past. Analytic thought dominates virtually all of the key "prestige" institutions in the United States and Great Britain. If you are not analytically trained, your chances of ever being hired (or even accepted to graduate school) in the philosophy departments at Harvard, Princeton, or Oxford are close to zero. Your chances of having a polite conversation about philosophy with analytic philosophers will even be somewhat in doubt.

By contrast, continental philosophy is influenced by key trends of the past century in Germany and France, especially the philosophies of Husserl and Heidegger. The best way to climb to the top of the pile in continental philosophy is not to argue heatedly about precise technical issues in philosophy using rigorous arguments, but rather to know a few foreign languages extremely well and have an outstanding command of the history of philosophy. If analytics see continentals as fuzzy dreamers lost in the history books and unable to make clear arguments, continentals return the favor by seeing the analytics as dry technicians who waste their time with nail-filing arguments over minor, artificial problems.

Unlike the analytics, continentals only rarely cite books or articles published in the past few years. Their view is that movement in philosophy consists not of step-by-step progress through professional journals and conference papers, but rather of massive paradigm shifts unleashed every once in awhile by rare great thinkers. For this reason, continentals are reluctant to reduce their philosophical heroes to a specific list of "arguments," since they have the instinctive sense that this procedure fails to do justice to the great figures. Indeed, the continentals maintain a permanent temple of great names, all of them much admired by the adherents of this school, whereas analytic philosophy does not seem to mind that it has produced so few thinkers who are likely to survive through the ages (Wittgenstein comes to mind, along with Saul Kripke and two or three other dark horse candidates). The great philosophers are admired by the continentals not for making valid arguments, but rather for their stylistic *brio* and their systematic visions of the universe.

I have described this situation at some length simply because any assessment of Heidegger's legacy needs to bear the current situation in mind. In one sense, analytic and continental philosophy were already unified from the start, since both are descendants of Kant's rejection of traditional metaphysics. Both focus on human access to the world (whether through perception or language) rather than the structure of the world itself. But in a second sense, the two schools remain hopelessly distant from one another thanks to all the cultural factors listed above.

Lately there has been much talk of "bridge-building" between the two schools. But this building of bridges is largely an illusion. It is of no interest whatsoever to the continentals, who often do not see the analytics as real philosophers in the first place. Meanwhile, it is acceptable to the analytics only because they have adapted such figures as Hegel and Heidegger to their own "mainstream" vision of philosophy. My own view is that this particular bridge can never be built. The end of the analytic/continental split will never come about through some sort of organized professional peace council, but will arrive only when both traditions have withered away in the face of something deeper that is somehow acceptable to the descendants of both camps. Martin Heidegger will not be able to fill this role, since the analytics have adopted him too late in life, and tend to misread him as a "pragmatist"—that is to say, as someone who believes that practice comes before theory, and that truth is defined by its significance for humans. Yet if Heidegger cannot serve as the basis for reconciliation in the philosophical world, certain elements in his thought may point the way to such a reconciliation—sometimes through his own innovations, but just as often through his obvious failures to innovate.

Looking Ahead

A new philosopher will inevitably have a somewhat confusing effect. It can sometimes be difficult to put one's finger on what makes a thinker important. Interpretations of a new philosopher are always somewhat unpolished and tentative. Heidegger was born over a century ago, yet by the glacial standards of philosophy, he is still our contemporary; at the same time, Heidegger is already regarded as a classic figure. In three or four centuries, we can assume that he will still be regarded as a classic, yet the various interpretations of his works are likely to be far less at odds with one another than is now the case. Our descendants will have the luxury of a better sense of what Heidegger actually accomplished and failed to accomplish in philosophy, since they will have a longer view of what came next.

In the year 2300, Heidegger will still be pored over by any number of scholars, and there may even be an occasional Heidegger renaissance now and then, as there is for most thinkers of comparable stature. Nonetheless, the live wires and loose ends of philosophy will have shifted elsewhere. Although we cannot know for sure where they will be, it is useful to make a rough guess as to which elements of Heidegger will survive and which are doomed to perish. The verdict of Emmanuel Levinas on Heidegger is that it would be foolish to want to return to a pre-Heideggerian philosophy, given all the new things Heidegger has seen. Nonetheless, Levinas continues, there is a profound need to leave the *climate* of his philosophy. Any new thinker of Heidegger's stature would most likely build on what he accomplished, while also discarding some of his unnoticed basic assumptions that block further insight. We should begin by briefly reviewing some of his accomplishments.

HEIDEGGER'S ACHIEVEMENTS

Above all, the critique of presence is an historic step in philosophy. For all the contributions made by Husserl, there are compelling reasons to accept Heidegger's criticism that Husserl reduced entities to their various surface profiles, and in this way caricatured or dehydrated the things of the world. By contrast, Heidegger was the champion of a "hermeneutic" approach in which things are interpreted as they emerge from a shadowy backstage instead of lying in lucid conscious awareness. This key step has had a profound impact, and if a bridge *could* be built between analytic and continental philosophy, it would probably be built with the aid of this hermeneutic approach. Even many analytic philosophers seem to be coming around to the view that all perceptions and statements emerge from some sort of dark background, whatever this might be.

Second, Heidegger has done a great deal to revive interest in the history of philosophy. I have suggested that his own historical readings are somewhat overrated, since they frequently amount only to Heidegger's monotonous discovery that some form of presence dominates all past philosophers, with the possible exception of the pre-Socratics. But at least Heidegger does not chirpily reduce his predecessors to four or five arguments that are then ruled "unsound" and quickly debunked, as too often happens among analytic philosophers. Heidegger is sensitive to the fact that all great philosophers arrived at their conclusions only through excruciating effort, so that equally painstaking effort is needed to reawaken their insights.

Finally, I would like to argue that Heidegger is someone who revolutionized our concept of *things*. It is true that he usually tends to focus either on human Dasein or on being itself. He often belittles individual things as "intraworldly entities" that would be uninteresting lumps of matter if not for human Dasein's use of them. Even so, Heidegger guides us through at least two dramatic moments in rethinking the thinghood of things. The first comes in the tool-analysis, where things withdraw from all presence into their silent function. The second comes in his concept of the fourfold, where things become quadruple mirrors, with each pole reflecting all the others. If it is true that Plato, Aristotle, and all later thinkers failed to capture the thinghood of things, Heidegger gives us our best hope to press forward toward the essence of things.

HEIDEGGER'S VICES

There are other virtues in Heidegger as well, but we have just enough time to turn to his vices. We should begin with politics, though the vice I have in mind is not the obvious one (we all hope that the philosophers of the future will not be fascist nationalists). The deeper problem may be Heidegger's lack of any political philosophy at all. This was noticed with especial clarity by his former student, the controversial Leo Strauss. Examine the list of the great speculative philosophers of the past century—and Strauss's list is a good one: Husserl, Heidegger, Henri Bergson, and Alfred North Whitehead. Now, notice the truly minimal role of political philosophy in these four figures in comparison with such past philosophers as Hegel, Locke, Spinoza, Hobbes, Aristotle, or Plato. All Hitler salutes aside, something has gone terribly wrong when thinkers of the stature of Heidegger or Whitehead almost completely avoid one of the major subjects of philosophy. The fact that four of the major thinkers of the century did avoid it suggests that this is a problem inherent in contemporary philosophy itself, rather than a remarkable coincidental weakness in all of them.

A First Objection to Heidegger

I would like to end this book with my two favorite objections to Heidegger. The first concerns the dominance of human Dasein in his philosophy. For Heidegger, at least most of the time, there is world only when Dasein is present. Only Dasein prevents hammers and trees from being dreary present-at-hand blocks of dull substance. Dasein's involvement with the things, Dasein's temporality, is what makes things interesting. But this seems obviously absurd. Although my own encounter with a fire is obviously rather different from a piece of paper's encounter with that fire, it does not follow that entities do not relate to one another at all when Dasein is absent. Although human Dasein's involvement with things brings them into an ambiguous interplay of presence and absence, the same is true of the things with respect to each other.

Dasein objectifies the fire only on the basis of using it or taking it for granted, and in this way the being of the fire is never fully used up by Dasein. But oddly enough, the same is true of paper and fire in relation to each other. The fire affects the paper only in a certain sense (flammable object), while never coming into contact with its other properties at all (blue, fragrant, and smooth object). In this sense, even inanimate objects objectify each other. Dasein's conscious awareness is not relevant at *this* level of the analysis, and only becomes relevant later, if at all. Heidegger needed to recognize that there is a sense in which objects withdraw from one another even in the absence of all Dasein.

A Second Objection to Heidegger

The second objection may seem even more unusual. Although Heidegger makes a breakthrough in defining the structure of things, he generally defines them only through their relations with *other* things. As he puts it, there is no such thing as "an" equipment. A thing's reality is found in its systematic relations with all other things in the environment. But to define all beings in terms of their systematic relations with other beings has at least two difficulties. First, it gives us no way to explain change, since nothing in the things is held in reserve beyond their current relations. In other words, if my house is nothing but a set of relations with other things, and if those relations adequately exhaust the whole of its being, why should the current relations in the world ever change at all? There needs to be some sort of tension between the things themselves and the way that things are perceived by other things. Otherwise, a static universe would be the natural result.

Second, Heidegger's theory of the system of entities gives no way to explain how there can be multiple simultaneous perspectives on the same entity. In other words, if a house is nothing but its relations, then the house is a completely different thing when viewed by a bird, by fifteen different humans standing in fifteen different places, and by a spy satellite. There is nothing that could possibly link all of these relations together in a common center. Heidegger needed to grant more independence to things from their environments. To his credit, this is what he finally began to do in his underrated 1949 Bremen lecture.

Concluding Remark

For those readers who go on to study the actual works of Martin Heidegger, plenty of other virtues and vices lie in store. Although Heidegger's books are often difficult, they can also be hypnotic, and are certainly never frivolous. Any time invested in reading him is time wisely spent, since he is never far from the central philosophical themes of our time. Further progress in philosophy will not be able to ignore his single great thought: being is not presence.

Suggestions for Further Reading

The following is a list of the major sources used for each chapter.

Chapter 1: Brief Biography

Rüdiger Safranski. *Martin Heidegger: Between Good and Evil.* Translated by Ewald Osers. Cambridge, MA: Harvard University Press, 1998.

This is a highly readable and detailed biography by one of Germany's leading public intellectuals. I have relied heavily on Safranski's book for the portion of chapter 6 covering Heidegger's actions as rector at the University of Freiburg.

Hans Dieter Zimmerman. *Martin und Fritz Heidegger: Philosophie und Fastnacht.* Munich: Verlag Beck, 2005.

This book is not yet available in English, but sheds such fascinating light on Heidegger's childhood and his misunderstood hometown that it is sure to be translated soon.

Chapter 2: A Radical Phenomenologist

Edmund Husserl. *The Essential Husserl.* Edited by Donn Welton. Bloomington: Indiana University Press, 1999.

A nice anthology of key writings by Edmund Husserl, with a brief and clear introduction by the editor.

Martin Heidegger. *Towards the Definition of Philosophy.* Translated by Ted Sadler. London: Athlone Press, 2000.

The long-needed translation of Heidegger's crucial 1919 lectures.

Martin Heidegger. *Phenomenological Interpretations of Aristotle.* Translated by Richard Rojcewicz. Bloomington: Indiana University Press, 2001.

A difficult but influential account of human life, seen as a three-fold structure of *Reluzenz, Ruinanz,* and *Larvanz.* This is definitely not the best of the early volumes to read first.

Martin Heidegger. *The Phenomenology of Religious Life.* Translated by Matthias Fritsch and Jennifer Anna Gosetti-Ferencei. Bloomington: Indiana University Press, 2004.

One of the most interesting of Heidegger's early lecture courses.

Martin Heidegger. *Ontology: The Hermeneutics of Facticity.* Translated by John Van Buren. Bloomington: Indiana University Press, 1999.

This was one of the key lecture courses in establishing Heidegger's reputation as the "hidden king" of German philosophy.

Chapter 3: Marburg

Martin Heidegger. *History of the Concept of Time.* Translated by Theodore Kisiel. Bloomington: Indiana University Press, 1992.

One of Heidegger's best lecture courses, and quite simply one of the most interesting things he ever wrote. This book is essentially a more lucid version of the first half of *Being and Time,* preceded by a lengthy celebration and critique of Husserl's phenomenology. It gets my vote as the ideal starting point for newcomers to Heidegger.

Martin Heidegger. *Basic Problems of Phenomenology.* Translated by Albert Hofstadter. Bloomington: Indiana Univ. Press, 1988.

A masterful example of Heidegger as a serious reader of the history of philosophy. This book helps establish what is most original in Heidegger's thought compared to the great philosophers of the past. Much of his other historical work is disappointingly slow and predictable in comparison with this *tour de force* of the Marburg years.

Martin Heidegger. *Metaphysical Foundations of Logic.* Translated by Michael Heim. Bloomington: Indiana Univ. Press, 1984.

An interesting interpretation of the German philosopher G. W. Leibniz, followed by a fascinating discussion of Heidegger's own concept of transcendence. This book also contains a moving impromptu obituary for the philosopher Max Scheler along with a mysterious section on "metontology," a concept that Heidegger never fully developed.

Chapter 4: *Being and Time*

Martin Heidegger. *Being and Time.*

This riveting masterpiece is now available in two different English translations. The earlier version, by John Macquarrie and Edward Robinson (San Francisco: Harper & Row, 1962) is still the translation I prefer. The more recent version was done by Joan Stambaugh (Albany: SUNY Press, 1996), who studied with Heidegger in Freiburg. It seems to me that Macquarrie and Robinson do a surprisingly good job of making the original work intelligible in English, and even their occasional strange new words have become comfortably familiar over time, making their translation a sort of King James Bible of Heidegger studies. While I am not convinced that Stambaugh brings the original text closer to us, some readers do prefer her translation.

Chapter 5: Freiburg before the Rectorate

Martin Heidegger. *Pathmarks.* Edited by William McNeill. Cambridge: Cambridge University Press, 1998.

This is a collection of numerous important essays and lectures. "What is Metaphysics?" is a masterpiece, one of the best short works that Heidegger ever wrote. It deals with the concept of nothingness. "On the Essence of Truth" already shows a weakening of Heidegger's philosophical energies following the failed 1929–30 lecture course.

Martin Heidegger. *The Fundamental Concepts of Metaphysics: World, Finitude, Solitude.* Translated by William McNeill and Nicholas Walker. Bloomington: Indiana University Press, 1995.

This fascinating 1929–30 lecture course is both the most promising and most disappointing course Heidegger ever gave. It contains a 100-page analysis of boredom and a further 100-page discussion of the differences between humans and animals. Yet the discussion of animal life soon collapses into a discussion of the as-structure, and tells us little about animals at all, despite a handful of juicy anecdotes drawn from biologists. The sections on boredom are magnificent.

Chapter 6: A Nazi Philosopher

Martin Heidegger. *Reden und andere Zeugnisse eines Lebensweges.* Heidegger *Gesamtausgabe*, Band 16. Frankfurt: Vittorio Klostermann, 2000.

This massive collection includes nearly 200 pages of speeches and documents from Heidegger's rectoral period alone. The entire volume is not yet translated into English, but someday surely will be. In the meantime, the works listed below may be a sufficient source for most readers.

Victor Farias. *Heidegger and Nazism.* Philadelphia: Temple University Press, 1991.

This is the book that reignited the Heidegger controversy in the late 1980s. Generally ridiculed by Heideggerians, Farias's book is not without importance, but is certainly not as skillful as Hugo Ott's study listed below.

Hugo Ott. *Martin Heidegger: A Political Life.* Translated by Allan Bluden. New York: Basic Books, 1993.

Ott contends that Heidegger's involvement with the Nazi movement was not just an ignorant mistake by a naive academic, and that Heidegger's commitment to the Party had deep roots. This book usually gets higher marks for scholarship than the more publicized work by Farias.

Gunther Neske and Emil Kettering. *Martin Heidegger and National Socialism: Questions and Answers.* Translated by Lisa Harries. New York: Paragon House, 1990.

This is a sourcebook in English for documents related to Heidegger's political scandal. It contains his famous interview for *Der Spiegel,* his 1969 television interview, and other relevant writings.

Chapter 7: Hermit in the Reich

Martin Heidegger. "The Origin of the Work of Art," in *Poetry, Language, Thought.* Translated by Albert Hofstadter. New York: Harper, 2001.

This is one of Heidegger's more celebrated short works, and a worthy contribution to the philosophical discussion of art.

Martin Heidegger. *Introduction to Metaphysics.* Translated by Gregory Fried and Richard Polt. New Haven: Yale University Press, 2000.

Long a favorite among readers of all backgrounds.

Martin Heidegger. "Hölderlin and the Essence of Poetry," in *Elucidations of Holderlin's Poetry.* Translated by Keith Hoeller. New York: Humanity Books, 2000.

This is Heidegger's clearest essay on Hölderlin, though not generally regarded as one of his most important. Those readers with especial interest in the Heidegger-Hölderlin connection are advised to try the lecture course *Hölderlin's Hymn "The Ister,"* translated by William McNeill and Julia Davis (Bloomington: Indiana University Press, 1996).

Martin Heidegger. *Contributions to Philosophy: From Enowning.* Translated by Parvis Emad and Kenneth Maly. Bloomington: Indiana University Press, 1999.

Despite a number of highly questionable translation choices— "enowning," "abground," and others—the English version of this book is approximately as readable as the original German, which is not meant to be high praise.

Martin Heidegger. "Nietzsches Metaphysik," in *Nietzsche.* Heidegger *Gesamtausgabe*, Band 50. Frankfurt: Vittorio Klostermann, 1990.

This volume is not yet translated. However, Heidegger's longer and better-known multivolume book on Nietzsche has been available in English for many years, and is a must-read for any student of Heidegger. It has now been compressed from the original four volumes down to two. See *Nietzsche: Volumes One and Two*, translated by D. F. Krell (New York: HarperCollins, 1991) and *Nietzsche: Volumes Three and Four*, edited by D. F. Krell (New York: HarperCollins, 1991).

Chapter 8: Strange Masterpiece in Bremen

Martin Heidegger. "Einblick in das, was ist," in *Bremer und Freiburger Vorträge*. Heidegger *Gesamtausgabe*, Band 79. Frnkafurt: Vittorio Klostermann, 1994.

This 1949 Bremen lecture cycle is the true second masterwork by Heidegger. For some reason, it has not yet been translated into English in full. But much of the material from the lecture did enter into later spin-off essays that are already available in English. See the entries that follow.

Martin Heidegger. "Building Dwelling Thinking" and "The Thing," in *Poetry, Language, Thought*. Translated by Albert Hofstadter. New York: Harper, 2001.

This pair of essays includes key themes from the portion of the Bremen lecture entitled "Das Ding."

Martin Heidegger. *The Question Concerning Technology, and Other Essays*. New York: Harper and Row, 1977.

This volume includes key themes from the portions of the Bremen lecture entitled "Das Ge-Stell," "Die Gefahr," and "Die Kehre."

Chapter 9: The Task of Thinking

Martin Heidegger. "Die Sprache," in *Unterwegs zur Sprache*. Pfullingen: Neske Verlag, 1959.

The English translation of this book is greatly abridged, and does not contain the essay on which I have focused. Readers may still enjoy the other essays on language in the English volume, *On the Way to Language*, translated by Peter D. Hertz and Joan Stambaugh (New York: HarperCollins, 1982).

Martin Heidegger. *What Is Called Thinking?* Translated by J. Glenn Gray. San Francisco: Harper, 1976.

This is certainly one of the clearest and best organized of Heidegger's late writings. However, Hannah Arendt's claim that the book is just as important as *Being and Time* is a stunning exaggeration.

Martin Heidegger. *Gelassenheit.* Pfullingen: Neske Verlag, 1959.

A portion of this work can be found in English in *Discourse on Thinking*, translated by John M. Anderson and E. Hans Freund (New York: Harper and Row, 1969). The dialogue on the country path is just as wooden as all of Heidegger's attempts to write dialogues, but readers may still find points of philosophical interest.

Martin Heidegger. *On Time and Being.* Translated by Joan Stambaugh. Chicago: University of Chicago Press, 2002.

Some of Heidegger's most important later essays are contained in this volume. In addition, the essay "My Way in Phenomenology" is a touching memoir by the elderly Heidegger.

Glossary

Angst. Angst is a rare fundamental mood directed toward being as a whole rather than toward specific beings. By confronting us with nothingness, Angst reveals the finitude of being, and leads us to wonder: "why is there something rather than nothing at all?" Heidegger claims that the mood of Angst is always with us, but most of the time it is "asleep," and is awakened only in special cases.

authentic/inauthentic. The more human beings interpret themselves on the basis of entities, the more inauthentic they are. The more humans interpret themselves in terms of their own inherent potentiality for being, the more authentic they are.

being. The question of being has been forgotten since ancient Greece, and Heidegger aims to revive it. As he puts it, the being of beings is not itself a being, but is something deeper than all specific beings.

being-in-the-world. Here the word "in" is not meant in a physical, spatial sense. For Heidegger, only humans exist in the world, fully open to it and affected by it. He denies being-in-the-world to physical objects, and even to animals.

beings as a whole/beings as such. This is similar to the classical existence/essence distinction. On the one hand, all things simply are (beings as a whole). On the other hand, all things are highly specific, each with its own characteristics (beings as such).

boredom. Like all fundamental moods, boredom is not just an inner psychological state, but reveals something about the world itself. In the 1929–30 lecture course, Heidegger describes three increasingly deep forms of this mood: we can be bored with entities, with ourselves, and finally with being as a whole.

care and concern. Human beings care about the world, which means that we are occupied with it and take it seriously as the site of our existence. By contrast, "concern" tends to be a negative word for Heidegger, since it refers to our absorption with entities in the world, and such absorption distracts us from the roots of our own existence.

chronos **and** *kairos.* Two different Greek words for time. Chronological time is measured on a clock. Kairological time refers to moments of important decision that cut time into before and after.

concealment and unconcealment (a.k.a. veiling and unveiling). Things are not just visible phenomena, but are partly hidden from view. We never gain an exhaustive understanding of things, but can only gradually draw them out of concealment by degrees, and this process never comes to an end. The Greek word for truth, *aletheia*, seems to point toward the same idea, since it means to draw something out of forgottenness.

curiosity. Always a negative word for Heidegger. Curiosity jumps from one superficial novelty to the next, and never cares to see anything deeply. By rapidly shifting between different interests, curiosity distracts us from our own being-in-the-world.

Dasein. A normal German word that usually means existence or presence. Heidegger redefines the term to refer solely to human existence.

de-severance and directionality. These two terms describe the spatiality of beings. De-severance translates the German *Ent-fernung*, which implies that distance is both increased and eliminated. When I view a distant building, for example, I am letting it be distant by noticing how far it is from me, yet I am also bringing it into intimate contact with myself by looking at it. Directionality means that everything we encounter belongs to a specific and limited region of our being, whether this region be physical or purely emotional. Although a bad mood isn't spatial, it still has directionality: for example, I might be in a bad mood over a quarrel with a friend, but can still enjoy a fine meal in a restaurant, since moods do not always spread throughout all regions of our lives.

destruction. Since humans do not view the world directly, but always through a tradition that they inherit (mainly the Greek philosophical tradition for Western peoples), we need to carefully disassemble that tradition in order to free ourselves from prejudice. This must indeed be done with great tact and finesse, even though Heidegger demands a "destruction of the history of ontology." The famous "deconstruction" of French philosopher Jacques Derrida (1930–2004) is modeled on Heidegger's concept of destruction.

enframing. Modern technology strips things of all mystery and places them in a gigantic framework that feeds on itself. Things become a mere stockpile or standing reserve.

event. For Heidegger, the world is filled with entities that always remain partly obscure. Things are events, not occurrences. They are not thoroughly graspable from the outside, and are never entirely exhausted by human thought.

fallenness (a.k.a. ruinance). Humans are absorbed by objects in the world, and in this way they forget themselves. Although Heidegger claims that this is true of all humans at all times, he clearly finds it to be more flagrant under modern technology than in the heroic period of ancient Greece. There are obvious theological overtones to this term, which refers to the fall of Adam and Eve from paradise.

hermeneutics. The philosophical theory of interpretation. Since things can never fully be seen, they must be interpreted. The term first originated in theology, in the context of Biblical interpretation.

idle talk. Much of what human Dasein says is not seen at first hand, but it superficially understood from the outside and passed along as a sort of gossip.

intentionality. The favorite notion of Brentano and Husserl that consciousness is always directed toward some object. Although Heidegger admires this insight, he also believes that intentionality reduces things to their accessibility to human thought. Husserl never asks about the *being* of intentionality, Heidegger claims, which means that Husserl never asks about the side of intentionality that withdraws from visibility.

metaphysics. Traditionally, metaphysics has always meant philosophical speculation about the ultimate nature of reality. Heidegger transforms it into a negative term. For him, it refers to types of philosophy that try to explain all of being in terms of one specific, privileged sort of being (such as atoms, God, or the human soul). As he sees it, all of Western philosophy from Plato through Nietzsche is dominated by metaphysics in the bad sense. Jacques Derrida, a great admirer of Heidegger, uses the word metaphysics in the same negative sense. Once in a while, Heidegger gives the word more positive connotations, but this is rare.

metontology. The name for a branch of philosophy that Heidegger proposed but never developed. It appears in his lecture course *The Metaphysical Foundations of Logic*. Whereas ontology talks about being as a whole, metontology was supposed to discuss specific regions of being, such as ethics and sexual difference.

nothingness. The experience of nothingness comes neither from concepts nor from grammatical negation in sentences. It can only be experienced in fundamental moods such as anxiety, being-towards-death, and a few others. Nothingness shows us that being is finite, by making us feel that being as a whole is slipping away from us.

objects and things. Heidegger generally uses "object" as a negative term and "thing" as a positive one. Objects are what we get when things are reduced to shallow caricatures of themselves. This happens through overvaluation of the theoretical understanding of things, but even more often through the essence of technology, which reduces things to mere objects.

ontic and ontological. "Ontic" is the adjective Heidegger uses to describe specific beings, while "ontological" is used to describe being itself. "Ontic" is almost always a negative term for Heidegger. It is generally uttered in tones of sarcastic contempt, often in combination with the word "mere." If told about the September 11 hijackings, for instance, Heidegger would probably say: "This supposed 'disaster' was a mere ontic incident. The essential danger to the West occurred far earlier, when being was forgotten."

phenomenology. The school of philosophy launched by Edmund Husserl's classic work *Logical Investigations* (1900–1901). It attempted to distinguish philosophy from science by abandoning all theories of how the world operates outside our perception of it, and focusing instead on describing the manner in which things appear to us.

present-at-hand. A negative term used by Heidegger to refer to things insofar as they are physically present, or visible to us by way of concepts. In both cases, things are reduced to their relations to other things, and stripped of any concealed, mysterious layer. Presence-at-hand is arguably the major enemy of Heidegger's entire philosophy. He believes that his greatest breakthrough in philosophy was to oppose the reduction of the world to presence-at-hand, which enabled him to renew the question of being.

ready-to-hand. This is the type of being possessed by tools. When things are ready-to-hand, they tend to withdraw from explicit view. At any given moment we use countless items of equipment: oxygen, floorboards, heart, kidneys, hammers, and computers. These things are rarely present to us. As long as they are working effectively, they tend to remain invisible. We usually notice them only when they break, turn up missing, or function badly.

the "they." For the most part, human Dasein does not see the world with its own eyes, but sees it the way others do. In phrases such as "they say that high school is the best time of your life," the "they" is no one in particular, not even a measurable 51 percent majority of individual people. It is an impersonal, inauthentic force that does our thinking and seeing for us. Only rarely do we break free of it.

thrownness and projection. Human Dasein is thrown into a world that it never chose (this would later serve as one of the key ideas of the existentialism of Jean-Paul Sartre and Albert Camus). Projection is the related and opposite term. We are not *only* thrown into an unchosen world, but also rise above that world and project our own possible choices onto it.

transcendence. Closely related to the term "projection." Humans are not just enmeshed in the world, but also rise partly beyond it, or transcend it. Otherwise we would understand nothing; even partial knowledge would be utterly impossible without some degree of transcendence.

truth. For Heidegger, truth is never a question of being correct or incorrect. Instead, truth is an endless process of unveiling or unconcealing. We gain an understanding of nature or history only gradually, by degrees. We never reach the point of having made all possible correct statements about any topic, since the world will always remain partly concealed from us.

withdrawal. Things are always partly concealed from us, never completely present-at-hand.

world. In *Being and Time*, "world" means that entities never exist in a vacuum, but are interrelated in a global system of references. Entities belong to a highly specific context from which they receive their meaning. In the essay "The Origin of the Work of Art," by contrast, "world" is the opposite of "earth." Earth is dark and concealed, but world is openly visible. Earth and world remain locked in a permanent strife that gives works of art their vitality.

Appendix:
Heidegger's Numerology

In Heidegger's writings there are frequent references to the four-fold (*das Geviert*) and occasional mentions of a fivefold (*das Fünffache*). At other times, he divides the world into two, three, or six distinct zones. These are never lists of different *kinds* of entities, a method completely foreign to his philosophy. Instead, they are structures of reality found in all places at all times, even if there are only special cases when they appear explicitly "as" what they are.

Heidegger often uses poetic terminology when he carves the world into parts. Understandably, this leads some of his more dismissive readers to accuse him of being arbitrary, precious, or self-indulgent. But in fact, each version of Heidegger's numerology is both rigorous and completely simple.

The one thing that usually remains unclear is how the separate zones of reality interact with one another. Heidegger often speaks of their relations using metaphors such as mirrors, weddings, dances, and songs. But his writings contain no crisp, lucid discussion of precisely how one zone is able to reflect another. Clarifying how this occurs may actually be one of the key problems for post-Heideggerian philosophy.

Given that all of Heidegger's numerologies arise from some combination of twofold and threefold structures, it is easy to imagine even more bizarre Heideggerian concepts that were never attempted, such as eightfolds, twenty-fourfolds, or ninety-sixfolds. Any non-prime number would be a feasible candidate. And prime numbers can also be obtained by adding an extra term and saying that it unifies all the others. (For example, the fivefold that Heidegger finds in Nietzsche comes from adding an overarching fifth term to organize the other four.)

Reading Heidegger without awareness of his recurring numerical structures is like doing chemistry without a periodic table. It promotes the notion that Heidegger is far more complicated than he actually is. In my view this prevents further progress in identifying how the various zones of the world interact, and causes readers to become distracted by a false diversity of terms throughout his career.

Twofold

Examples: absence/presence; veiled/unveiled; concealment/unconcealment; ontological/ontic; sheltering/clearing; ready-to-hand/present-at-hand; being/beings; things/objects; earth/world; thrownness/projection; state of mind/understanding.

What It Means: The world is an ambiguous duality. Visible surfaces conceal a hidden depth that can be brought to light only gradually, and never completely. This is Heidegger's fundamental insight, the one that makes all the others possible. It arises from his revision of Husserl's phenomenology, in which entities are nothing but their appearance in consciousness, with no independent life of their own. In many ways, Heidegger's entire philosophy can be read as an attempt to restore independence to things. This becomes clear from 1949 onward.

Note that in the essay on art (1935) "world" functions as a term for unconcealment in opposition to hiddenness, but in his other numerologies "world" often refers to reality as a whole rather than just a half or a third of it.

Examples of a Different Twofold: something at all/something specific; beings as a whole/beings as such; formalization/generalization; the "not" of nothingness/ the "not" between being and beings. These examples are different from the previous list, since all of them occur on the levels of concealment and unconcealment alike. For example, the visible hammer in my hand is both something at all and something specific, and the same holds true of the invisible hammer that is silently used until it malfunctions. The intersection of the two separate dualities is what gives rise to Heidegger's fourfold.

Threefold

Examples: past/present/future; world/finitude/solitude; world-relationship/irruption/attitude; that which is interrogated (*das Befragte*)/that which is asked about (*das Gefragte*)/that which is to be found out by the asking (*das Erfragte*).

What It Means: Without exception, threefolds are always connected to Heidegger's theory of time. All three temporal aspects are contained in every instant. "Past" is simply the world that confronts me without my having chosen it. "Future" is simply the way that my own understanding of possibilities configures the world that is given to me. (Two people thrown into the same environment will nonetheless understand the situation in different ways.) These do not refer to actual past and future moments in the history of the world, but are the two opposite faces of the present.

In other words, Heidegger's threefolds are simply a twofold structure of absence and presence, with a third term added at the center to unify them.

Fourfold

Examples: earth/sky/gods/mortals; the pre-worldly something/the world-laden something/the formal-logical objective something/the object-type something; pre-theoretical dealings with things/pre-theoretical circumspection/the figure of things/the outward look of things.

What It Means: The fourfold is generated by crossbreeding the absence/presence difference with that between something at all and something specific (also known as beings as a whole vs. beings as such). The four aspects are found in all entities at all times, and do not refer to four specific kinds of entities. For example, a piece of dirt contains all four terms, not just earth. The same holds true of a cloud (not just sky), a person (not just mortals), and the Hindu pantheon (not just gods). Although Heidegger believes that the fourfold only becomes the fourfold in special cases, such as temples and peasant shoes as opposed to plastic cups and nuclear power plants, the four are there at all times for all entities.

Both earth and gods are concealed and can only be approached by hints, whereas mortals and sky refer to explicit visibility.

But in a different way earth and mortals belong together, since both refer to the unity of beings as a whole (the earth is always one, and the anxiety of mortals in the face of death reveals being as a unified whole). Meanwhile, gods and sky also belong together insofar as both refer to the plural qualities in the essence of each specific being, although the gods are concealed and merely hint, while sky is explicitly present for us.

The second set of examples comes from the year 1919, when the young Heidegger crossbred his own distinction between concealed and revealed with Husserl's difference between formalization (any thing is something at all) and generalization (any thing is a specific something). This is the moment when Heidegger emerged as an independent philosopher.

The third set of examples comes from Heidegger's 1922 lectures on Aristotle. The pre-theoretical environment has two aspects (dealings and circumspection, *Umgang* and *Umsicht*), while the visible world also has two aspects (figure and outward look, *Gestalt* and *Aussehen*).

These early fourfold structures gradually passed into silence for Heidegger, but were explicitly revived in the crucial 1949 Bremen lecture, which paved the way for the so-called later Heidegger of the 1950's. His famous discussions of language and technology are actually derivative of his theory of the fourfold nature of entities.

Historical Note: Fourfolds arise continually throughout the history of philosophy. The most famous is Aristotle's four types of causation: material, formal, efficient, and final. Although Heidegger denounces past fourfolds as reducing things to mere presence, there is a great deal of continuity between the fourfolds of Aristotle, Heidegger, and other philosophers.

Fivefold

The Only Example: eternal return/will to power/superman/nihilism/justice.

What It Means: The fivefold is found only in Heidegger's writings on Nietzsche. It arises from taking a fourfold structure and adding a fifth term, *justice*, to unify the others. This is a bold move on Heidegger's part, since justice (*Gerechtigkeit*) is far less common in Nietzsche than the other four terms. But it does allow Heidegger to allude to the pre-Socratic philosophy of Anaximander, who held that justice will destroy all opposites over the course of time.

Historical Note: Heidegger believes that Nietzsche remains trapped in metaphysics in the bad sense, even though he brings it to completion. For this reason, Heidegger claims that the four key terms in Nietzsche remain just as mired in traditional metaphysics as Aristotle's four causes.

Nonetheless, there is a direct correlation between Nietzsche's and Heidegger's fourfolds. Eternal return is earth (concealed beings as a whole). Will to power is gods (concealed beings as such). Superman is mortals (revealed beings as a whole). Nihilism is sky (revealed beings as such).

Sixfold

The Only Example: playing-forth/the last god/grounding & echo/the ones to come/the leap. (Better translations of some of these terms are possible; for convenience I deliberately use those found in the existing English translation. The German words are *Zuspiel/der letzte Gott/Gründung* & *Anklang/die Zukünftigen/Sprung*. See the diagram on page 121 above.)

What It Means: The sixfold is found only in the mysterious *Contributions to Philosophy*. It results from placing two threefold temporal structures in counterpoint to one another. The reason for doing so is that *Contributions* aims to describe two separate beginnings of philosophy: the ancient Greek beginning, and the only other possible beginning, whose time has not yet come. Each of these two beginnings is dealt with by means of a threefold temporal structure, whose doubling yields the sixfold.

After World War II, Heidegger speaks almost exclusively of fourfold structures.

Index

absence, 1, 2, 49, 79, 92, 118, 149, 162, 180, 181
absorption, 66–67, 71, 106, 174
adequation of mind and world, 70, 91
Adorno, Theodor, 13
aletheia, Greek word for truth, 92, 138, 153, 154, 174
ambiguity, 27, 85, 93, 115, 122
  as fallenness of Dasein, 69
  as twofold structure of reality, 2, 138, 162, 180
analytic philosophy, 157–59
Anaximander, 125, 183
animal life, 79, 84, 85, 88–90, 127, 144, 168, 173
anti-Semitism, 95, 100–101, 119, 124
anxiety (Angst), 35, 55, 70, 72, 73, 74, 83, 88, 107, 133, 173, 176
a priori, original sense of in Husserl, 40–41
Arendt, Hannah, ix, 8, 9, 10, 37, 101–2, 171
  death of, 13
  Heidegger's literary agent in America, 13
  Heidegger's lover, 8
  inspiration for major works, 8, 55
Aristotle, 6, 16, 26, 28, 37, 43, 47, 53, 74, 89, 148, 154, 161, 162, 182, 183

failed to think the essence of the thing, 130, 131, 132, 138
as-structure, 74, 85, 90, 112, 133, 140–41, 168, 179
atomic bomb, 129, 131, 136, 139
Augustine, Saint, 24
authentic/inauthentic, 60, 71, 72, 73, 74, 76, 77, 98, 173, 177

Basic Problems of Phenomenology (1927), 37, 44–50, 166
Baumgarten, Eduard, 102
Beaufret, Jean, 12
beginnings of philosophy, first and other, 118, 119, 120, 121, 122
being, 32, 42, 43, 56, 88, 99, 108–9, 117, 122, 138, 144, 146, 154, 155, 173, 176, 180
  being is the emptiest and most universal concept, 57
  being is not presence, 1, 4
  being is time, 1, 56–57
  as different from beings, 45, 50
  history of, 129
  humans as shepherds of, 140, 141, 148
  as opposed to becoming, appearance, thinking, and ought, 109
Being and Time (1927), 1, 3, 9–10, 16, 19, 30, 37, 38, 44, 49,

185

55–78, 99, 102, 127, 136,
148, 166, 167, 171, 177
Dasein's temporality, 73–78
death, conscience, and
resoluteness, 71–73
fallenness and care, 66–70
great work of philosophy, 55
question of being, 57–60
tool-analysis, 60–66
being-in-the-world, 61, 68, 70, 72,
88, 91, 173, 174
beings as such and as a whole, 81,
82–83, 88, 90, 91, 98,
125–26, 173, 180
Bergson, Henri, 162
Berlin, 9, 16, 97, 102
beyng (*Seyn*), 93–94
Birle, Erika (foster daughter), 11
Black Forest, 35, 36
Heidegger's hut, 8, 38, 76, 96,
103
Blochmann, Elisabeth, 10, 102
boredom, 79, 81, 84, 85–88, 127,
137, 168, 173
boredom with being itself
(finitude), 87–88
boredom with ourselves (solitude),
87
boredom with world, 86
held in limbo, 86, 87, 88
left empty, 86, 87
Braque, Georges, 12
Bremen, site of 1949 lectures, 12,
125, 127–41, 143, 163
Brentano, Franz, 6, 16, 154, 175
*Psychology from the Empirical
Standpoint*, 16
Brock, Werner, 101
"Building Dwelling Thinking"
(1951), 128, 170
Bultmann, Rudolf, 8, 37

Caesar, Friedel
biological father of Hermann
Heidegger, 7
Camus, Albert, 70, 177

care, 75, 173–74
Carnap, Rudolf, 80, 84
Cassirer, Ernst, 10
categorial intuition, 39–40, 42, 45,
48, 50, 154
Catholic Church, 6, 7, 17, 95, 103
The Vatican, 103
Celan, Paul, 13, 96
Char, René, 12
Christianity, 60, 102
chronos and *kairos*, two forms of
time, 31, 34, 56, 174
clearing, 3, 83, 91–94, 118, 133,
138, 153, 180
concealment, 71, 83, 91–94, 120,
122, 132, 133, 134, 138,
139, 146, 153, 174, 177,
180, 182
concentration camps, 95, 96, 100,
136, 137, 139
concern, 66, 173–74
conscience, 72, 73, 75, 77
continental philosophy, 157–59
Contributions to Philosophy
(1936–38), 105, 117–22,
127, 169, 183
not Heidegger's second great
work, 122
curiosity, 68–69, 174

Danger, The, 138–39, 140
paired with saving power, 140
Dante, 115
Darwin, Charles, 47
Dasein, 2–3, 25, 28, 30, 31, 33, 35,
43, 45, 48, 49, 50, 52, 53,
55, 58, 59, 60, 61, 62, 64,
66–67, 68, 71, 73, 74, 76,
82, 83, 85, 88, 90, 99, 101,
102, 106, 107, 116, 130,
155, 161, 162, 174, 175, 176
average everydayness of, 60, 67,
74
as historical, 73–75
needs terror to be saved, 88
poses the question of being, 56

as temporal, 3, 51
who not what, 60
death, 35, 55, 71, 72, 73, 75, 77,
    121, 133, 139, 176, 182
Democritus, 48
Spiegel, Der (German magazine), 13,
    169
Derrida, Jacques, ix, 59, 174, 175
Descartes, René, 38, 46–47, 84
destruction of the history of
    ontology, 59–60, 174
Dilthey, Wilhelm, 23, 75, 114
distance and nearness, 128–29, 134,
    135, 137, 138, 145
Duns Scotus, 7, 28

earth
    in the fourfold. *See* fourfold
    in the work of art, 109–12, 120,
        150, 151, 177, 180
echo (*Anklang*), key term of sixfold,
    119, 120, 121, 122, 183
"End of Philosophy and the Task of
    Thinking" (1964), 151–53
enframing (*Gestell*), 135, 137, 138,
    139, 175
environment, 23, 25–26, 27, 32–33,
    35, 90
epochs of being, 118, 139, 140
equipment, 22, 35, 49, 62, 63, 64,
    74, 110, 129, 133, 163, 176
    equipmental strangeness, 23, 35
    for-the-sake-of-which, 64–65
    towards-which, 6⁻
eternal return, 148
    as key term of fivefold, 125–26,
        134, 182–83
ethics, 53, 176
event, 22, 24, 33, 117, 119, 121,
    122, 131, 135, 138, 146,
    175, 175
existence and essence, 27, 43, 44,
    60, 82, 125, 133, 134, 173

facticity, 25, 26, 27, 30, 61

fallenness, 44, 71, 73, 175
fate and destiny, 76, 77, 107, 116
Fichte, J. G., 113
finitude, 81, 83, 88, 107, 181
Fink, Eugen, 20
fivefold structure, 118, 124–26, 132,
    179, 182–83
formal indication, 27, 90, 135
formalization and generalization, 27,
    182
Förster-Nietzsche, Elisabeth, 124
founding (*stiften*), 112, 117
fourfold structure, 12, 83, 85, 108,
    118, 124, 125, 129–41, 143,
    144, 145, 146, 161, 179,
    180, 181–82, 183
    as crossing of two dualisms,
        132–33, 180
    as dance, 131, 179
    as mirror-play, 129, 131, 132,
        133, 134, 138, 143, 179
    as wedding, 131, 179
    earth and gods in Hölderlin, 116
Fraenkel (Jewish professor), 101
Freiburg, 6, 7, 8, 9, 13, 19, 20–36,
    38, 54, 67, 78, 79–94, 96,
    109, 128, 154, 165
    decimated by bombing raid, 11
    occupied by French forces, 12
Freud, Sigmund, 17
Führer
    Germany needs leaders, 98
    title for Hitler used by Heidegger,
        10, 99, 101
Fundamental Concepts of Metaphysics
    (1929), 9, 79, 84–91, 127,
    167, 168, 183
future, 2, 29, 57, 74, 75, 80, 83, 88,
    91–94, 98, 118, 120, 121,
    133, 181

Gadamer, Hans-Georg, 10, 14, 35,
    56–57
    Truth and Method, major work, 56
Galileo, 46, 47
gods. *See* fourfold

Goethe, J. W. von, 115
Gontard, Suzette ("Diotima"), 113, 114
Göttingen, 8, 19, 128
Greece, 13, 36, 43, 57, 59, 60, 78, 92, 98, 105, 111, 119, 124, 136, 139, 149, 173, 174, 183
Gröber, Conrad, Archbishop, 6, 11
Grounding (*Gründung*), as key term of sixfold, 119, 120, 121, 122, 183

Hartmann, Nicolai, 9
Hegel, G. W. F., 113, 153, 159, 162
  Phenomenology of Spirit, 55
Heidegger, Elfride Petri (wife), 7
Heidegger, Fritz (brother), 5–6, 11, 101
Heidegger, Hermann (son), 7, 11
Heidegger, Jörg (son), 7, 11
Heidegger, Marie (sister), 5
Heidegger, Martin
  actions as Rector in Freiburg, 100–103
  Aristotle, supposed link with, 16
  athletic abilities, 6. 13
  biography, 5–13
  charismatic teacher, 10, 13
  committed Nazi, ix, 10
  "early" and "late" periods, 15
  greatest twentieth-century philosopher, 14, 157
  health problems of, 6, 7
  "hidden king" of German philosophy, 8, 9
  Husserl's successor in Freiburg, 9, 35, 54
  lack of publications, ix, 9
  loyal to the Kantian tradition, 3
  overrated as historian of philosophy, x, 166
  personality, 13–14
  phenomenologist, 6, 8, 28, 86
  physical appearance, 13
  prolific writer, ix
  psychological problems after war, 11
  rector of University of Freiburg, 10
  stable temperament of, 123
  tainted by political scandal, 14
  view of self as key figure in philosophy, 28, 59–60, 130
  writing style, 14
"Heil Hitler!"
  Nazi salute used by Heidegger, 101
hermeneutics, 32, 160, 175
  hermeneutic circle, 58
Hevesy, Georg von, 101
Hilbert, David, 19
history, 122
  as axis of the fivefold structure, 126
  importance for Heidegger's philosophy, 23
  as sheltering darkness, 121
History of the Concept of Time (1925), 4, 9, 37, 38–44, 166
Hitler, Adolf, 10, 11, 95, 988, 99, 101, 102, 105, 162
Hobbes, Thomas, 162
  notion of being as copula, 44–45
Hölderin, Friedrich, x, 39, 105, 112–17, 123, 124, 131, 136, 139, 140, 169
  biography, 113–14
  danger and saving power, 116, 140
  "Homecoming," 114–15
  lecture courses on hymns, 113
  patron poet of the ones to come, 122
"Hölderlin and the Essence of Poetry," 113, 169
Homer, 115
"Horst Wessel Song" (Nazi anthem), 97
Husserl, Edmund, 4, 6, 7, 8, 9, 12, 21, 23, 25, 32, 33, 40, 44, 50, 54, 56, 58, 78, 95, 96, 100, 101, 102, 134, 153,

154, 158, 160, 162, 165, 166, 175, 180, 182
biography, 16–20
called to Freiburg, 19
criticized by Heidegger, 21, 24, 38, 39, 50
critique of mind-body problem, 61, 63
death of, 20
dedication of *Being and Time* to, 55
defense of objective truth, 70
discouraged in early years, 18
editor of Ye*arbook for Phenomenology and Phenomenological Research*, 9, 19
end of Freiburg career, 20
funeral not attended by Heidegger, 10, 20
Ideas I, 19
Logical Investigations, 18, 19, 176
Lutheran conversion, 17
mentor of Heidegger, 16
personality of, 17, 19
psychologism, critique of, 18
rejection of transcendence, 51
student of mathematics, 17, 18
Husserl, Gerhard, 100

idle talk, 34, 68–69, 73, 175
Insight Into What Is (1949), 12, 13, 83, 125, 127–141, 170, 180, 182
intentionality, 17, 18, 30, 39, 41, 175
interpretation, 1, 2, 32, 34, 58
intimacy (*Innigkeit*), 112, 115, 145–46
Introduction to Metaphysics (1935), 105, 106–9, 169
irruption, 80, 181

Jaspers, Karl, 8, 9, 13, 99
death of, 13

fired due to Jewish wife, 10
report on Heidegger to Denazification Commission, 11
Jews, ix, 7, 8, 10, 13, 16, 20, 95, 96, 100, 102, 157
jug, as example of fourfold, 129–31, 134, 136
justice (*Gerechtigkeit*), key term of fivefold, 125–26, 182–83

Kant, Immanuel, 3, 40, 44, 51, 134, 147, 148, 152
Kant and the Problem of Metaphysics (1929), 39
Kepler, Johannes, 46, 49
Klostermann, Vittorio (publisher), x
Kreutzer, Konradin, 149
Kripke, Saul, 159
Kronecker, Leopold, 16

language, 68, 115, 116, 140, 143–46, 147, 182
"language speaks," 144
"Language" (1950 essay by Heidegger), 143–45, 170
last god, the, (*der letzte Gott*), as key term of sixfold, 119, 120, 121, 122, 183
Latin language
as inferior to Greek, 107, 134
the leap (*der Sprung*), as key term of sixfold, 119, 120, 121, 122, 183
Leibniz, G. W., 37, 47, 50, 167
Leipzig, 16, 123, 124, 128
"Letter on Humanism" (1947), 12
letting-be, 90, 149
Levinas, Emmanuel, ix, 10, 160
wartime experiences of, 96
Locke, John, 162
Logical Investigations. *See* Husserl, Edmund
Löwith, Karl, 113

Macquarrie, John, translator, 34, 65, 167

Marburg, 4, 8, 9, 32, 35, 37–54, 79, 128, 129, 166

Marburg School, neo-Kantian philosophers, 37

Marx and Marxism, 152, 157

mass media, 67, 137, 150, 151

Messkirch, hometown, 5, 13, 149
  damaged in bombing raid, 11

metaphysics, 136
  history of, 107, 159
  as negative term, 54, 93, 94, 107, 108, 125, 132, 151, 153, 175
  as positive term, 108

Metaphysical Foundations of Logic (1928), 50–54, 167, 175

metontology, 53, 85, 167, 175, 176

Möllendorf, Wilhelm von, 100, 103

moods, 18, 67, 73, 83–84, 106, 107, 173, 174, 180

mortals. *See* fourfold

Mussolini, Benito, 105

"My Way in Phenomenology" (1963), 153–54, 171

nature, 29, 62, 107, 138, 177
  as *physis*, 107, 111

Naumburg, 113

Nazism, ix, 2, 5, 7, 10, 20, 73, 95–103, 105, 109, 119, 124, 168

Newton, Isaac, 47, 49, 70

Niemeyer, Hermann, 154

Nietzsche, Friedrich, x, 39, 55, 76–77, 82, 101, 105, 107, 114, 119, 123–26, 134, 147, 148, 152, 175, 179, 182, 183
  biography, 123–24
  The Birth of Tragedy, 124
  Thus Spoke Zarathustra, 124

Nietzsche (work by Heidegger), 124, 170

Nietzsches Metaphysik (1936–37), 123–26, 132, 170

nihilation, 52, 82, 120

nihilism, 138, 182–83
  as key term of fivefold, 125–126, 134

nothingness, 9, 31, 50, 52, 55, 80–84, 87–88, 106, 107, 167, 176, 173

numerology, 118–19, 179–83

Nuremberg (Nürnberg), 97

objects
  as things reduced to presence, 29, 129–31, 134, 135, 173, 176, 180

"On the Essence of Truth," 79, 91–94, 128
  begins period of stagnation, 79–80, 167

"On the Way to Language" (1959), 143–45, 170–71

ones to come, the (*die Zu-künfti-gen*), as key term of sixfold, 119, 120, 121, 122, 126, 183

ontic, 58, 132, 176, 180

ontological difference, 45, 48, 93–94, 118, 145, 180

ontotheology, 48, 54

Ontology: Hermeneutics of Facticity (1923), 32, 166

opening/opennness, 91, 93, 98, 120, 126, 153

organs, 88–90

"Origin of the Work of Art" (1929), 39, 105, 109–12, 120, 169, 180

outward look (*Aussehen*), 25, 33, 62, 130, 137, 138, 148, 181, 182

Parmenides, 149

past, 2, 29, 57, 74, 75, 80, 83, 88, 91–94, 98, 118, 120, 121, 133, 181

Paul, Saint, 24

Petzet, Heinrich Wiegand, 12, 14, 128

Phenomenological Interpretations of
Aristotle (1921–22), 28, 166
phenomenology, 4, 16, 18–20, 21,
23, 27, 43, 72, 154, 155,
166, 176, 180
epokhe, "bracketing," 41–42, 43
ignores history too much, 33
intuition of essences, 32
misses the question of being, 42,
44
radicalized by Heidegger, 8, 9, 16,
21, 28, 32, 38–44, 50
reduction, 42
"to the things themselves" motto,
42
Phenomenology of Religious Life
(1920–21), 24, 166
philosophy
as irreducible to its content, 15–16
as perpetual crisis, 24–25
it does something with us, 106
Plato, 26, 37, 43, 47, 102, 107, 124,
125, 148, 152, 161, 162,
175
failed to think the essence of the
thing, 130, 131, 132, 138
Meno, 58
Republic, 99
Sophist, 57
Plato's "Sophist," (Heidegger lecture
course of 1924–25), 37
playing-forth (*Zu-spiel*), as key term
of sixfold, 119, 120–21, 122,
183
poetry, 116, 117, 144
all art is essentially poetry, 112
as greater than science, 107
possibility, 60, 68, 76, 88, 173
presence-at-hand (*Vorhandenheit*), 2,
3, 45, 57, 59, 61, 62, 63, 70,
76, 77, 89, 91, 92, 110, 117,
118, 120, 131, 139, 140,
145, 146, 162, 176, 177, 180
present, 2, 29, 34, 49, 50, 57, 74,
75, 79, 80, 88, 92, 98, 106,
109, 118, 120, 121, 129,
135, 136, 144, 145, 151,

153, 155, 161, 162, 163,
180, 181
pre-Socratic philosophers, 119, 161,
183
projection, 49, 98, 118, 176, 180
public reality, 33, 34–35, 60, 62, 77

"Question Concerning Technology"
(1953), 128, 170

rectorate, 80, 95–103, 105, 165
readiness-to-hand (*Zuhandenheit*),
49, 62, 63, 75, 89, 176, 180
releasement (*Gelassenheit*), 93, 151
resoluteness, 73, 74, 93
revealed, 83, 91–94, 133, 139
Robinson, Edward (translator), 34,
65, 167
Rosenberg, Alfred, 10
hanged at Nuremberg, 97
ruinance, 30, 31, 44, 166, 175
philosophy as countermovement
to, 30–31

Safranski, Rüdiger, 127, 165
Salomé, Lou von, 124
Sartre, Jean-Paul, 12, 43, 70, 177
Being and Nothingness, 12
Scheler, Max, 154, 167
Schelling, F. W. J., 113
Schiller, Friedrich, 113
Schmitt, Carl, 97
Schopenhauer, Arthur, 147–48
science, 21, 44, 58, 80, 81, 107,
138, 146, 147, 148, 152,
157, 176
according to phenomenology, 4,
17
fails to do justice to life, 23–24
fails to think the essence of the
thing, 130
objectifies pretheoretical
experience, 46–47
"science does not think," 146

"Self-Assertion of the German
    University," (1933), 10,
    97–99
sending, 118, 139
sexual difference, 53, 176
Shakespeare, William, 115
sheltering, 83, 91–94, 111–112, 118,
    119, 121, 133, 141, 146,
    180
"Sieg Heil!"
  Nazi salute used by Heidegger, 10,
    97, 101, 102
sixfold structure, 118, 120, 121,
    124, 179, 183
sky. *See* fourfold
Socrates, 58, 102, 113
soil, 149–50, 151
solitude, 87, 98, 181
Sophists, 58
Sophocles, 115
Soviet Union, 2, 11, 108, 109, 147
space, 35, 65, 135
  de-severance, 65–66, 174
  directionality, 65–66, 174
Spinoza, Baruch, 38, 162
spirit, 98, 99
Stalin, Joseph, 11
Stambaugh, Joan, translator, 167
standing reserve (*Bestand*), 135, 136,
    137, 138, 139, 140, 175
Stanley, Wendell, 150
Staudinger, Hermann, 102
Stein, Edith (Saint Teresa Benedicta),
    95–96
stockpile, 135, 136, 137, 138, 139,
    140, 175
Strauss, Leo, 162
strife, 110–12, 120, 122, 125, 126,
    177
Stumpf, Carl, 17
superman, 148
  as key term of fivefold, 125–26,
    134, 182–183
swastika, 97, 113
system of meaning, 26, 62, 63,
    64–65, 74, 75, 86, 89, 136,
    163, 177

technology, 2, 12, 108–9, 116, 118,
    120, 126, 128, 129, 137,
    138, 139, 140, 141, 144,
    146, 150–51, 175, 176, 182
temporality, 1, 28, 29, 30, 34, 45,
    48, 49, 50, 51, 52, 57, 59,
    68, 73, 74, 75, 77, 84, 102,
    109, 116, 118, 162
  ecstatic temporality, 49
Teresa of Avila, Saint, 95
Thales of Miletus, 48
thanking, 148, 149
"they, the" (*das Man*), 34, 67, 69,
    72, 73, 177
"Thing, The" (1950), 128, 170,
    176
things, 107–8, 129–31,134, 135,
    138, 145, 161, 162, 174,
    175, 176, 180
  contrast with objects, 29
  interplay with world, 144
Third Reich, 96, 102, 103, 105, 143
threefold structure, 84, 90, 98, 99,
    102, 118, 179, 181
thrownness, 68, 72, 88, 98, 118,
    177, 180
time, 26, 27, 28, 48, 49, 174, 181
  as horizon of the question of
    being, 56
Todtnauberg, 8
tool-analysis, 18, 61, 83, 88–90,
    91–94, 110, 136, 161, 176,
    177
  broken tools, 63, 83
  greatest moment of philosophy in
    century, 63
Towards the Definition of Philosophy
    (1919), 7–8, 15, 16, 20–24,
    38, 82, 98, 117, 146, 165,
    182
Trakl, Georg, 144–46
  "A Winter Evening," 144
tranquillization, 67, 71, 77
transcendence, 35, 46, 50, 51, 52,
    74, 75, 83, 167, 174, 177
truth, 70, 79, 91–94, 119, 139, 154,
    176

question of the truth of being, 120, 121
Tübingen, 113, 114, 128
Tugendhat, Ernst, 13
the turn (*die Kehre*), 53, 139–41
twofold structure, 118, 179, 180

uncanniness, 70, 150
understanding, 67, 73, 180
United States of America, 2, 13, 108, 109, 147

Van Gogh, Vincent, 110
veiling and unveiling, 3, 91, 118, 154, 174, 177, 180
Virgil, 115

Wagner, Richard and Cosima, 124, 147
Wagner, Robert (Reich Commissioner), 100
waiting, as attitude toward the desolation of being, 109, 118, 141

Weierstrass, Carl, 16
"What is Called Thinking?" (1951–52), 146–49, 171
"What Is Metaphysics?" (1929), 9, 79, 80–84, 167
Whitehead, Alfred North, 162
will to power, as key term of fivefold, 125–26, 134, 182–83
withdrawal, 1, 4, 117, 139, 147, 151, 162, 177
Wittgenstein, Ludwig, 159
Wolff, Christian, 37
world, 61, 63, 76, 84, 86, 88–90, 98, 110, 145, 148, 177, 181
    as center of fourfold, 131
    interplay with thing, 144
    strife with earth, 109–12, 120, 122, 180
World War I, 7, 20, 77, 124
World War II, 6, 11, 123, 146, 183

Zubiri, Xavier, 10

CPSIA information can be obtained
at www.ICGtesting.com
Printed in the USA
JSHW020829270520
5906JS00002B/83

9 780812 696172